Too Hot for (

Too Hot for Comfort
War Years in China 1938–50

Bill Ream

Bill Ream

EPWORTH PRESS

British Library Cataloguing in Publication Data

Ream, Bill
Too hot for comfort: war years in
China 1938–50.
1. Methodist Church——Missions——China
2. World War, 1939–1945——Religious
aspects 3. World War, 1939–1945——
Personal narratives
I. Title
266'.7'0924   BV3415.2

ISBN 0–7162–0442–8

First published 1988
by Epworth Press
Room 195, 1 Central Buildings
Westminster, London SW1

Printed in Great Britain by
Richard Clay Ltd, Bungay, Suffolk

Contents

Preface

I am grateful to former colleagues for their help, in particular to Donald Childe, Bert Alton, Charles Steel and Winifred Penny, all of whom checked part or all of the original typescript and made helpful suggestions and some corrections, and, not least, to Dr John Rose who not only read the whole but kindly wrote for me the extraordinary story that forms Appendix A.

Nearer home, relatives and friends have offered encouragement and I am most grateful to my wife, Mary, who typed the whole book from my atrocious handwriting and to Mrs Brenda Brake who retyped it to stricter professional standards. My thanks too to our son and daughter who, many years ago, listened to some of the contents of this book as bed-time stories and demanded more. Finally I acknowledge my indebtedness to the Hong Kong Government for a blanket and two exercise books which I took from the store of the Queen Mary Hospital for use in the Japanese Internment Camp and for which I would be very willing to pay if anyone can establish a valid claim to the money. I used the exercise books to record the details of Camp life. The blanket was not only warm but must have been of excellent quality because it is still in use by my wife as an ironing blanket.

A word about the Chinese place names. When writing about South China I have allowed myself to keep to the Cantonese pronunciation and romanization in which I spoke and wrote. Where, however, I thought that the reader might wish to refer to a modern atlas I have put in brackets the new 'P'in Yin' phonetic script which was authorized by the Chinese Government in 1979. An exception is in the final Appendix where I have put the P'in Yin spelling first and then, in brackets, the romanized form that was familiar to all 'foreigners' in earlier years.

vii

1 · Slow Boat to China

The P & O passenger liner, SS *Rawalpindi*, was tied up in the London docks. She'd had a tough ten days with the rattling of cranes and the thumps and cries of the dockers as they first unloaded her and then prepared her for yet another voyage. The hawsers that held her to the quay chafed her and hurt her pride for she knew that she was made for the seas of the world. In spite of all she maintained a solemn dignity as she towered over men and machines, sheds and offices and all other boats and craft in her vicinity. But the day of her release had come. The cargo, the stores, the passengers with all their luggage were stowed away and her siren sounded to tell all around that she was off.

It was to be a memorable voyage. We sailed quietly down the Thames by daylight and through the English Channel in the dark. We tried to give names to the various groups of lights that betokened English seaside resorts. In the meantime Neville Chamberlain, the British Prime Minister, was corresponding with Hitler and Mussolini. On 28 September 1938 he was addressing the House of Commons when a message was received from Hitler proposing a meeting at Munich the following day. The Munich crisis was on. Our ship was ordered to pick up a British admiral from Marseilles which we duly did and were diverted to Malta. We began to reckon up the places we would have liked to visit on that island had the opportunity been offered but it was made clear that there would be no going ashore. Valletta harbour looked fascinating and indeed beautiful in the sunshine. Even with the talk of possible war we never envisaged the ruin that was to befall the island nor the subsequent courage of its inhabitants.

After Malta we were back on course with reminders all the way to Hong Kong of the far flung nature of the British Empire which was so soon to break up to make way for the Commonwealth. Everywhere along the route were the signs of British sovereignty, British business, British influence, together with the Navy and

1

the Army in tropical kit. Suez seemed a bewildering Vanity Fair even though a large, modern Department Store represented its more normal life and concerns. We made our acquaintance with the gully-gully boys but otherwise, possibly with a view to our morals and certainly with a view to our pockets, we played it cool. The passage through the Suez Canal was fortunately made by daylight in a long convoy and it fascinated those of us who were making the trip for the first time.

A month's voyage in a passenger liner to the Far East is so unknown in these days of plane travel and jet lag that it is worth explaining briefly what it was like. Class distinction was *de rigueur* in that we travelled second class and were not allowed on to first class accommodation though friendly first class passengers were allowed to visit us. After leaving the Mediterranean behind, steerage passengers were taken on board and camped out on an open deck. A dispensation was allowed in the field of religion. All were welcome to the Sunday morning service in a first class lounge and I remember attending a regular prayer meeting in a first class cabin.

The first class passengers had English or Scottish stewards while we had Goanese. Roderiques was the name of mine and he did what I thought was a first class job. They had fresh water in their baths; we had sea water and special soap. They were allowed to linger in their bath; we were allotted ten minutes. They had a longer menu but we had no complaints about ours. I am not sure whether we shared our three-man orchestra with them but it served us well. We had films and dancing in the evenings and the most popular dance was the Lambeth Walk which was then fairly new. We had a good time at night and we also enjoyed ourselves by day playing deck quoits and deck tennis. The P & O deck tennis I found to be of a good deal higher standard than my post-war experience with Elder Dempsters boats to West Africa, but then the passengers to India and the Far East had a much longer journey. The final of the men's singles was always a tussle worth watching. Later, on a boat of the Elder Dempster line, I won some goldplated cufflinks. I never stood a chance on the P & O boats. There was also the opportunity of unhurried reading and preparation for the work that lay ahead of us but all in all it was a time of relaxation made all the more enjoyable because there was no other way to get to India, China or Japan anyhow.

Behind it all there was an indefinable air of romance, especially strong for the younger passengers. There was the romance of travelling to the Far East for the first time, the romance of visiting strange places heard of since childhood and only half accepted as real, the romance of the day to day life of a big ship tempered only by the rolling of the Bay of Biscay, the romance of seeing flying fish and porpoises in the sea and Buddhist temples and oriental markets on the land. There was also a romantic strain of another kind. The ship's officers were not, I think, as open to admiration as some expected but with the passengers it could be another matter. A temporary and perhaps warm friendship was one thing but we were also told the cautionary tale of a fiancée who was sailing to be united in marriage with her betrothed and who fell in love with someone else on board and married him instead. Indeed someone said that they thought that this voyage was the first time for some years that our missionary society had allowed its single men and single women to sail on the same ship. I have often wondered whether this was true but never had the courage to ask.

Then of course there were the ports of call, sometimes for as much as two or three days to take on water and provisions and to discharge and ship cargo. On the Red Sea we had several hours on shore in Aden. It was a Sunday and we went to a service in the Anglican church on the sea-front which had somewhat old electric fans stirring up the air for us – a token of the palliatives that civilization had brought to the tropics. The service over, someone told us the story of a British consul who was stationed on Perim Island not far away and slipped away to spend a few days in London. It was one of those strange almost unbelievable co-incidences that in Oxford Street he bumped into his superior who was on leave.

On to Cochin in South India – I believe that in those days the P & O boats called at either Cochin or Bombay but not both. It looked a small place but in any case there was no going ashore. It was a matter of off-loading and loading cargo only. At Colombo, however, we had a whole weekend and I was able to stay with Morris Kedward, a Handsworth theological college friend, at

Wesley College. He took me round the main sights of the city and we then left the city behind in a visit to seaside Mount Lavinia which was one of the tourist spots. I was glad of the opportunity to meet my fellow Methodist missionaries in Colombo. Those were the days when, by and large, the main missionary societies (after tragic earlier experiences especially in West Africa) looked after the men and women they sent out better than many business firms. I met the redoubtable Chairman's wife, a delightful person but with a Victorian sense of discipline. She insisted that all local colleagues should meet each weekday evening to play tennis at their manse; only the most daring thought up excuses.

Penang on the Malayan peninsular was our next port of call. In small groups we toured this deliciously green town and environs and visited the large and lovely Buddhist temple for which the place was famed. There were interesting signs of inter-faith influence. A series of paintings about the life of the Buddha reminded us of the Stations of the Cross and the carving of the lotus flower on the palms of the hands of the statues of the Buddha seemed linked with the marks of the nails on the hands of Christ.

At Singapore we had a stay of two days and again I was fortunate in that I had been invited to stay with a friend in the Presbyterian Mission whom I had known at Cambridge and who lived near us at home in New Barnet. He showed me round the pre-war Singapore which was bustling with life but not as phrenetic as it is now. I remember that he assured me that in Singapore they exercised complete control over the weather. It was always sunny by day and only rained at night. No doubt the information came with a few grains of salt but it may well have been true at that time of the year. At least it was true for the two days I was there!

So on to the South China Sea. Two things stand out in my memory. The first is that a ship's officer told us that American ships in those parts (we were passing one at the time) were often set on the automatic pilot and relied solely on the look-out on other ships to keep out of the way! An exaggeration no doubt but a reminder of the Britisher's niggling suspicion of our American cousins which has persisted through the generations. The other, very different, piece of news came over the radio that the Japanese army had taken Canton and that the city was burning. A number of us on the boat were expecting to go on from Hong Kong to various stations in Kwangtung province and further north and east. I myself was to be stationed at a boys' Middle School at Fatshan, some ten miles west of Canton where we had a large compound with a hospital as well as the boys' and girls' schools. This took the wind out of our sails and seemed to balance the Munich scare at the beginning of the voyage. The Japanese had invaded Manchuria in 1931. The 'Shanghai War' (or 'Incident') was in January 1932. In 1937 the Japanese launched a major attack on China. Chiang Kai-Shek withdrew his headquarters from Nanking to Hankow and finally in 1938 to Chungking in the far West, still on the Yangtse and beyond the reach of the Japanese navy but not of the air force. Nevertheless the optimistic hope was always there that the Japanese would be halted somewhere, and the fall of Canton, so near to Hong Kong, was a specially significant triumph for the Japanese. Incidentally a similar unrealistic optimism was very much alive in Hong Kong at the time of Pearl Harbour in 1941 when the Japanese had been on Hong Kong's border for nearly three years and finally attacked and took the colony.

2 · Learning Chinese

But it was Hong Kong at last which has one of the best and most beautiful harbours in the world. The barren rocky island (the original Hong Kong or 'Fragrant Harbour') was acquired by the Crown in January 1841. Later, in 1861, Kowloon peninsula on the mainland side of the harbour was acquired, and later still, in 1898, there was the lease of the 'New Territories' which expires in 1997. In that year the whole of the Colony will become part of China under terms and conditions that have been painstakingly worked out with the Government of China. It could not by any stretch of the imagination claim to be democratically governed but it has been well governed over the years considering the varying circumstances it has had to face. Under the Governor there is the Executive Council which consists of ex-officio and nominated members. The ex-officio members are also on a Legislative Council which consists of other ex-officio members and unofficial members nominated by the Governor. With the vital help of District Officers the colony was governed in a way that satisfied most of the Chinese population who were, generally speaking, quite content to let the British have all the headaches of government while they got on with their own businesses and money-making. There was a naval dockyard and other industry including shipbuilding and an ever-growing number of factories, but its prosperity always rested on the fact that it was a Free Port where you could buy almost anything from almost any part of the world.

I did not have to leave British waters because my destination was the South China Language Institute which had escaped from Canton in time and found refuge on an island by the name of Cheung Chau (Dumbell Island). It has a sort of narrow waist where there was a fishing village with most of the farming land nearby and the harbour on the sheltered side. It took about an hour for the ferry to reach it from Hong Kong. The southern, rocky promontory of the island was not suitable for farming and here some of the missionary societies and one or two businessmen had built solid bungalows either for their residence or for holiday homes. These were scattered over the area but there was a communal spirit, especially now that the Language School had arrived and held its classes in the communal hall. In many ways it was a delightful place. There were one or two bathing beaches and social events were organized, not the least of these being country dancing in the house of a retired businessman, Harold Smyth, who was generous and patient in the extreme but a martinet as a master of ceremonies. I can still hear his voice ringing out, 'Reel, Ream, reel,' and I was not often the only one who was out of step. He made an invaluable contribution to the morale and fellowship of us all. The students at the Language School represented a considerable number of countries – USA, Canada, New Zealand, Australia and Britain come to mind – and

6

a number of missionary families were there in safety, having left the husband to carry on his medical, educational, church work or whatever, in the sorely troubled parts of South China. There was also peace and time for dreaming in our various abodes and twice a week we could see the Imperial Airways sea-plane bringing in mail from England. The post worked on the 'all up' system which meant that all first class mail now went by air. An ordinary letter cost 1½d!

But we had work to do. We had to learn to read and write Chinese characters, a few each lesson to start with and later on there were the standard 'Thousand Characters' which I believe were first collected by a Chinese working for the YMCA among Chinese labourers in Europe during the First World War. Even more important we had to learn to speak Cantonese, which meant mastering the nine 'tones' which are a special difficulty of the Cantonese dialect. In those days the church and the Bible Societies quite rightly stressed the importance of using the language of the people and the New Testament and 'Pilgrim's Progress' had been translated and printed in Cantonese so that I had both to speak and read Cantonese. Even then, though, the Chinese Government of the day was pressing for the sole use of the 'national language' (sometimes loosely called 'Mandarin') both for speech and for writing so that the idea of writing Cantonese fell by the wayside. The 'national language' was that spoken by most Chinese so that there was a standard written language based on a standard pronunciation which educated Chinese in the South have now accepted. However, Cantonese are non-conformist in many ways and the Cantonese dialect has persisted strongly to the present day and is spoken by ordinary folk as well as by many overseas Chinese, e.g. in Chinese restaurants in this country. The dialects of other areas such as Fukien and Wenchow have shown an equally stubborn resistance.

So we were plunged into Chinese at the shallow end. The students at the Language Institute produced their own magazine of which I have only one copy left. Someone wrote, perhaps a little despairingly, 'There is only one way to learn Cantonese perfectly and that is to be strapped to the back of a Cantonese mother at an early age.' Too true! There were nine teachers, all

Chinese of course. They were a patient lot with us 'foreigners' and they had to be because we were not in a Chinese-speaking environment. We talked among ourselves in English – in different dialects! I can still hear the voice of our teacher ringing in my ears: 'Wan tsaap,' he would say over and over again, the English translation being 'revise' and the American 'review'. He was dead right. We had to keep at it. I see that in the same magazine there was also a little ditty addressed to the Principal:

> O Mr Sz To,
> What shall I do!
> I've learnt a hundred characters
> But I've learnt a swear word too.

In 1939 I was able to spread my wings a little. I had visited Hong Kong itself a number of times especially at weekends. I felt reasonably at home in the place and had seen some of our Methodist work there. There was the old English Methodist Church on the way to Happy Valley. In connexion with this there was the Sailors and Soldiers Home in Hennessy Road rehoused in more commodious premises in 1929 with an extension in 1934. This was strategically situated at the beginning of Wanchai's red light district. Opposite was the Chinese Methodist Church opened as recently as 1936 – a remarkably fine building in a modern Chinese style. The church proper seated seven hundred people and it was always crowded on Sunday mornings. In 1938 (the year I had arrived) there were four hundred baptisms! It was the minister of this strong church, the Rev. Wong Chung-Hoi, who gave me my Chinese name on my first visit and it was in this church that I was ordained at the 1940 Synod.

It was an education in itself to see the Tao Fong Shan Christian Institute at Shatin in the New Territories. This was a sort of Christian Buddhist monastery which in its day was a pioneer project in a field that has since become so important – the need to create understanding and fellowship between the world's major religions. In 1922 Dr Reichelt, a Norwegian missionary and an expert in Chinese Buddhism, founded here at Shatin this Christian Mission to the Buddhists. Buddhist priests were welcome to stay for weeks or months to talk and lecture on their own faith and to

8

hear the Christian faith expounded. All shared in a community of study, meditation and fellowship. Outside the chapel (itself a fine exposition of Christian faith and worship) there was a free-standing piece of sculpture depicting a white lotus flower growing out of the mud of the pond (in Buddhist symbolism purity growing out of the sin and dirt of the world) with a surmounting cross growing out of the lotus flower. It summed up well all that this unique mission (still going strong in the 1980s) stood for.

During the summer I was also able to see Canton for the first time. Much of it had been spared but whole areas, especially in the centre, had been devastated and burnt. Japanese bombing must have accounted for a part but most of what I saw had been destroyed by the Chinese army when it retreated – the so-called 'scorched earth policy'. My main port of call was our Methodist compound at Fatshan (Foshan) some ten miles away where the school buildings were standing, for the most part unoccupied. These were one side of the narrow street that ran from the town into the country. On the river side it was very different. The hospital there was at full stretch and here I stayed with an English doctor and his wife, John and Dorothy Rose, who were old Cambridge friends. It was my first opportunity to see the work of a hospital from the inside. It was well established and with well trained staff. It had been founded by Charles Wenyon in 1881 who was both a medical doctor and an ordained minister. In his youth he had tramped across Australia and America, earning his keep by lecturing and doing odd jobs. He had been to Fiji and some of the South Sea Islands, to Scandinavia and across Eastern Europe before settling in a Lancashire Methodist circuit where he heard the call to serve in China. In 1896 he wrote a book, *Across Siberia on the Great Post Road*, which described his journey home to England just before the Trans-Siberian Railway was opened and in its preface he claimed to be 'perhaps one of the last Englishmen to travel the whole distance from the Pacific coast to the Ural Mountains in the old-fashioned way'. He travelled in the spring and summer of 1893. Truly there were giants in those days. He left China in 1900 and the work of the hospital had by then been firmly established, built on a new site in 1890. In 1939 it boasted a Nursing School which was known throughout the

9

Province for its high standards. It owed much to the succession of English matrons and especially Kathleen Banks who has only recently died. The generation of Chinese sisters in 1939 was excellent.

I was able to do the rounds with the doctor and also allowed to watch operations. The daytime was interesting but the time I liked best was the evenings when I followed the doctor on his rounds. Sometimes of course there was an emergency but, when all was quiet, there was then to me, and I think to the patients, a special sense of peace. Operations had been carried out, treatment had been given, dressings and medicines had duly been dealt with, prayers had been said and the lighting dimmed. All that could be done had been done and the sister in charge was perhaps sitting at her table keeping her watch, checking up on reports by the light of the paraffin lamp (electricity was not yet available). I can only describe the atmosphere as a kind of divine benison in which the doctors and the nurses and indeed the whole staff had played their allotted part – which was not surprising as this was what the hospital was all about.

Outside the hospital things were very different. There was great poverty, distress and hunger among the people left behind. All those with money had gone. The Japanese planes had a free run of the skies and we often saw them on their way to bomb some village which had incurred their wrath. Mothers unable to feed their babies exposed them in public places and some in the narrow streets outside the hospital – all girl babies. In a quiet way an orphanage was started on the school compound, The Springfield Children's Home, and looked after by Agnes Chan, the Chinese matron of the hospital – in her spare time! How a year or two later they escaped to free China is a story too long to tell here. In 1982 the third foundling discovered the name of Frank Evison, the missionary who had rescued her, and wrote a letter to him in England to thank him and tell him that she was happily married and was living in North-West China, thereby spanning a gap of forty-four years.

In those days before Pearl Harbour the British, the Americans and 'foreigners' generally were neutral. In our Methodist church the handing-over of leadership and authority to the Chinese members had already gone a long way. Circuits, church schools and hospitals were under trained and qualified Chinese leaders, and the first Chinese Chairman of the District was soon to be appointed. It so happened, however, that the property was still registered at the British Consulate and the ancient privileges of extra-territoriality still lingered on. There was therefore a sudden rash of Union Jacks on our buildings which was a protection for the Chinese just as British passports were of some help to missionaries and other individuals. They were removed even more hurriedly when Pearl Harbour happened, but such is life! Not that the Japanese were particularly friendly or helpful. In order to apply for a travel permit, for example, we learnt that it was necessary to go to the Gendarme headquarters early in the morning. We would be told that it was unfortunate that the officer who issued permits was away for the day. We would reply that we were sure that he might be back in a short time and we would wait. Wait we did, often for hours until some time in the afternoon we got our permits. It was a great lesson in patience that backed up the parable of the importunate widow. During this time a wise and experienced ex-China missionary, H. B. Rattenbury, came to Canton from our Missionary Society Head-quarters in London to visit us. He was allowed to travel to Canton but wanted in particular to come to Fatshan. He asked our Chairman, Donald Childe, to call at the headquarters of the Gendarmerie in Canton to secure the necessary permit. He was told that it was not possible for him to go because of military manoeuvres. 'H.B.R.' sent him back a second and then a third time. By then the Japanese Commander's patience was distinctly strained. In broken English he shouted, 'How many times must I tell you that you cannot go?' H.B.R. decided on a fourth attempt and this time accompanied Donald Childe and sat himself down gazing fixedly at the Commander in complete silence. Permission was suddenly granted and the two were taken to Fatshan in a Japanese launch as VIPs. H.B.R.'s face and substantial frame were notoriously reminiscent of the Buddha as seen in so many temples and rumour soon had it that the Japanese Commander had been startled to see an incarnation in front of his very eyes.

The same summer I also managed a brief holiday on Laan Tau

(Lan Tao). Laan Tau is another island in British waters and larger than Hong Kong island itself. Very little development had taken place. It had a fascination of its own and over the years I got to know parts of it well. It is basically a great mass of rock with the main peak over 3,000 feet. It has a Buddhist monastery tucked away in a hollow on its northern slopes and a number of small fishing villages clinging to its many inlets. Farmers cultivate the valleys where streams have washed down soil over the ages. At Tai O on its western shore looking towards the Pearl River there were, and probably still are, great salt pans. I was to learn both to love and fear this island, but my first visit was delightful. Missionary Societies had developed a slope at the top of the mountain as a holiday and rest resort. They had built stone shacks with sturdy 'typhoon' shutters to withstand the fiercest wind. Often wives and children were then spending half the summer there and were joined by their husbands for their shorter holiday break. At 3,000 feet the air was cool and invigorating and did wonders for those who could get away to this camp from the hot humid summer of South China.

The development was simple, even primitive, but effective. Roughly at the middle of the long line of shacks was the community hall which served as mess, concert hall and church. A stream had been tapped higher up and the water piped as far as the community hall. A pool a short way down one of the slopes had been deepened as a swimming pool. One owner, then retired, had even built a stone wall outside his shack which sheltered a bit of a garden. The normal approach was by a trail from Mooi Woh, a village on the eastern shore where a ferry called daily and brought mail and food and other necessities for the village and the camp. A regular coolie service up the mountain kept us in close touch with Hong Kong. Here I met missionaries of many nationalities and denominations. A few had spent most of their working lives in China. There were ministers doing pastoral and evangelistic work in the churches aided by a growing number of ordained Chinese ministers and catechists; there were doctors and nurses, school teachers, university lecturers and professors including a number belonging to Lingnan University outside Canton, an American foundation going back to 1893. All in all it was a rich fellowship indeed.

3 · A School in Exile

In February 1940 I was sent as chaplain and English master to the Wa Ying Boys' School which was refugeeing in a very different part of Laan Tau. My Chinese was woefully inadequate but at least I was in a community where only Chinese was spoken. Some of the teachers of course knew English and could help out when necessary and one of them was allocated to me as my language teacher.

The school had been opened originally in Fatshan in 1914 on a site that had been the town's execution ground and was therefore easier and cheaper to buy. Its sister school, the Wa Ying Girls' School, had been established on the same compound at Fatshan in 1923. Both schools had succeeded in evacuating to Hong Kong in the summer of 1938 when Japanese bombing was being intensified. The Girls' School found a home in the Chinese Methodist church. The Boys' School had been allowed by the Hong Kong Government the use of an old 'yamen' at Tung Chung on the north side of Lan Tao Island. This yamen went back to days long before Hong Kong was ceded to the British and had been the headquarters of a District Magistrate or Mandarin in the old Imperial days. Oddly enough some old cannon lying here were found to have been made in Fatshan. The story was still told of how a mandarin in those far off days received an Imperial Government grant to support a thousand soldiers with head-quarters in the Yamen. By way of a check he had to parade with them once a year on the mainland. Somewhat ingeniously he kept a mere hundred and the rest of the money. Just before the annual Parade he would enlist men from this and other villages, fit them out with uniforms, give them two or three days' drill and parade with his one thousand men. The men received a small gift of money and a free trip to the mainland and in this way everybody was happy.

The yamen was partly in ruins but the stone walls still stood though with great gaps, probably where the stones had been used by villagers. The imposing stone entrance was intact and over the entrance, actually on top of the wall, was a restored building which was the Manse. Small though it was, perhaps twenty feet long, it was divided into study, bedroom, kitchen and toilet. This sufficed for me (a bachelor); it also had to suffice for my predecessor, Leonard Hickin, and his wife. Len Hickin had made a fine contribution to the life of the school while at Fatshan, having been trained as a scientist and engineer. In particular he had organized a foundry and metal work for which the school had become noted. At Tung Chung I found that he had already laid a pipeline for water from higher up the valley which was pumped by water power directly into the yamen. The whole of the interior of the yamen had been cleared of rubble and cheap bamboo matting classrooms and dormitories had been erected. It was all that could be done in the circumstances but as it happened they served our time there. The chapel for which I was particularly responsible was also built of matting but against a sound outside wall. Many were the times when I had to don some protection in heavy rain (often at night) to see where the rain was coming in and in particular make sure that it was not running on to our harmonium. School assemblies, each morning, were of course in the open air.

The boys and masters had been able to do a certain amount of public health work in the village but not much. The villagers' outlook had not apparently changed for centuries – certainly going back before the cession of their island along with other islands and Hong Kong itself to the British a hundred years earlier. They were used to doing things in their own way and accepted flies and rubbish as part of life. Moreover they did not think much of the invasion of their privacy by the school. Their attention was drawn to stagnant water and when it was explained to them that malaria was due to a certain kind of mosquito which bred in such water and attacked human beings, their looks made it quite clear that they had never heard such rubbish in their lives. They knew that there were European influences around and no doubt attributed this idea to some European fairy tale.

The villagers must have developed a certain immunity to

14

malaria. They would not have survived down the years otherwise. Be that as it may, the school was certainly not immune. I had heard that soon after they reached Tung Chung more than half the school had gone down with malaria. It took the healthy all their time to look after the sick. But they pulled through and when I arrived there was a refugee Chinese nurse. Presumably they had prophylactic tablets but I don't know what. Boys and masters were under strict orders to wear mosquito stockings after dusk. These were all home-made from calico or some other material and covered knees as well as ankles. The anopheles mosquito (and I presume all mosquitoes) lies low in the daytime but at dusk emerges like Dracula thirsting for blood. Its favourite hunting grounds are ankles and elbows of human beings. The boys had long-sleeved shirts which helped to protect the elbows. It was by no means full protection but it certainly helped. Incidentally women missionaries long before had pioneered this ungainly stocking (shorter stockings or long socks were in use by men). Later some claimed that two pairs of nylon stockings served as well but I was never in a position to judge whether or not they were sacrificing themselves as hostages to fortune in the interests of good looks. The school persevered for another twelve months after I joined it but in the end it was malaria that drove us out. We got one or two very ill boys to a hospital in Hong Kong and, alas, one or two died. The isolation of the place also ruled out any long stay. We had to move once more.

Hong Kong was packed with refugees. We found it possible, however, to find accommodation by dividing the school into two. In September 1940 the Junior School was established in a large building in Kowloon on the mainland side of the harbour. The Senior School which I joined found a delightful site further out in the New Territories at Shatin. There was a large house with an open space which could be used as a playing field and a two-room bungalow the other end. The masters and boys made themselves at home in the house and outbuildings. Dormitories, classrooms and a workshop were fitted out and our itinerant chemistry lab set up once more. One room of the bungalow became the chapel and I lived in the other room and had the use of the flat roof for a bit of peace and quiet, not least on Sunday afternoons. The bungalow was isolated from the school and it was ideal for private talks with any boy or master who wanted to come along. The situation was between an inlet of the sea and the main road and railway line that ran to the frontier. It was to prove a dangerous place later on but we enjoyed the fresh air and the proximity to Kowloon and Hong Kong. It was like old times to be able to get on a train again. I had my own private blessing in that I was able to get a daily pint of the Bishop of Hong Kong's goats' milk! R. O. Hall was his name. He had a country place or farm at Shatin where one of his many practical projects was an attempt to interest the Chinese in goats.

By now I was much more at home in the school and interested to see how it was run, especially under these refugee conditions. I was impressed at staff meetings with the wise and understanding way in which the teachers discussed individual boys and their problems. There were just over a hundred and twenty boys in this senior part of the school. The matter of discipline was unusual. Corporal punishment had some time before been banned by the Chinese (Nationalist) Government except in primary schools. The understanding was that students over twelve or thereabouts had to accept reasonable orders and regulations or leave the school. The only regular enforcement of discipline was by giving bad marks which went on the boy's record. These were read out at morning assembly and the boy had to see the Acting Head (the Head himself was in charge of the Junior part of the school) during the break. Much of the discipline was carried out by the boys themselves. Thus each class had a monitor who was responsible to the master for good order and who had to keep his class quiet during prep. There was no official supervision by the masters except during the teaching periods themselves, though a different master was on general duty each day and one master was in charge of the teaching side of school life.

Morning assembly was in the open air. A routine day would begin at 6.45 with assembly before a portrait of Sun Yatsen, the founder of the Chinese Republic, and all bowed their heads as a mark of respect and loyalty. There would then be a hymn, prayer, reading and brief address by one of the Christian masters. Assembly was followed by ten minutes' PT. Several boys from Christian families refused to bow because for them to bow was to worship. Their conscientious objection was upheld and I do not remember any difficulty about this with either boys or masters. It reminded me of the tragic clash – on a much vaster scale – between the Vatican in Rome and the Jesuits in China in the seventeenth century. Part of the trouble was that the Jesuits allowed their converts to continue the traditional ceremonies that were held in honour of Confucius and their ancestors. Most Jesuits accepted the ruling of Matteo Ricci, the first Western missionary to establish himself in Peking, that these rites had only a civil significance and that Christians could honourably continue to join in them. The Pope ruled otherwise. For what it is worth, I reckon that the Jesuits were right in their day and the school in ours!

Lessons continued according to the timetable. One feature that I remember with special appreciation was that each class was put under one or two teachers who were called 'class-advisers'. I was promoted to their ranks when it was felt that I could get by language-wise. The object was for masters and boys to get to know each other without a master-student relationship. Sometimes we would play games, sometimes sit and talk (away from the school grounds), sometimes go to the railway station to 'yam ch'a' (drink tea). The period must have been very elastic for on one occasion I was taken by my class for a picnic in a nearby valley on a really glorious day. We did not climb high enough to be able to drink the water from the stream but we made a fire and boiled some duck eggs. These, with bread and jam, peanuts and a nasty looking mess made from beans, provided an enjoyable meal which lasted me until breakfast next day. On another occasion I was taken to see a Buddhist monastery where there was a monk on view who claimed to have been locked up in his room for over four years. Local gossip claimed that he did not remain locked up at night!

The syllabus included one lesson a week on Religious Instruction. These were taken by the Christian teachers and also by Bert Alton who came in from Hong Kong. After some months it was found to be more satisfactory to divide the boys into three groups according to their knowledge and experience of Christianity. Each group was divided into A and B classes, making six in all.

Outside the classroom the Students' Association became active. One boy was in charge of sport, another of literary studies, another of social activities and so on. Then there was the Student Christian Association which arranged Wednesday morning prayer meetings and various discussion groups, sometimes at night beside the sea by the light of a couple of paraffin pressure lamps. One interesting 'prayer meeting' to which I was invited consisted, apart from prayer, of a violin solo, two anthems, a hymn, scripture readings and a short address by one of their number. At the beginning of one term they arranged a questionnaire in which the boys were invited to express their opinions on Christianity. It was interesting that a number said that their initial interest in Christianity derived from the higher standards and morale of Christian hospitals and the fact that church leaders and missionaries stayed behind when the Government people fled (they were thinking of the Japanese occupation). At one point, with the approval of the acting Head, I ran a series of meetings on 'The Bible and Christian Doctrine', which, as I look back, must have sounded, and probably was, more than a little heavy. Ten boys gave in their names and fifteen turned up, most of them non-Christians. I mention this as an example of the real and uninhibited interest in Christianity and the church.

A third Association was the YMCA, which was something of a misnomer in that it had nothing to do with the international YMCA with which we are familiar. It was, however, concerned with the outreach of Christian discipleship and arranged such forms of social service as village work, a club for school servants and musical performances. Two of its officers rejoiced in the title of 'odd-job men', an office which I soon realized should be a 'must' on all committees.

Unobtrusive guidance from time to time by members of staff no doubt helped but all these activities were carried on by the boys themselves. It was good training in self-government. The boys by and large seemed to me to be more mature than English boys of similar ages. One reason was obviously the ordeal of separation from parents and families, real hardship and the uncertainties of refugee life. It was also true that some of the boys who had fled with the school from the Japanese were pursuing their studies beyond the normal school-leaving age and so added a bit of senior stiffening. Staff and students had gone through traumatic experiences and there was an underlying trust between them.

It is worth mentioning that only about a quarter of the boys were Christians and only a small number of the rest became Christians while at the school. The percentage of Christian masters was higher but not more than some 50%. I am sure that this mix of Christian and non-Christian was healthy and indeed ideal. It meant that in religious, as in other matters, there could be open and unselfconscious discussion.

We maintained what links we could with the Junior School in Kowloon. They were hemmed in with buildings and did not have the games facilities that were available at Shatin, where baseball, basketball, fistball, swimming and rowing were all enjoyed. We welcomed parties and individuals who were able to join us for some fresh air. They were also able to help us in various ways. On one such occasion when we needed help for a summer school at Shatin they sent us a new master they had taken on straight from Training College in Hong Kong. It happened that on a day's visit to Hong Kong it got late and he decided to spend the night in his own room in the Junior School, not knowing that it had been temporarily lent to the drawing master and his wife. He was not surprised to find his room locked and did not want to wake anyone up for the key at that hour. Having noticed that the window was slightly open he climbed in – and fell on top of the drawing master's wife. Varying descriptions were given of the shriek she let out but it woke up most of the school and it took a little time to determine what had happened. It was an embarrassing start for a new recruit but the story scored a top rating when it reached Shatin. On a more serious note, we had joint Conferences and Retreats and we took advantage of the facilities that Hong Kong offered such as exhibitions of teaching material and regular gatherings of Heads and deputy-Heads from Hong Kong schools.

My own specific jobs were to teach English and act as School Chaplain. English essays were always interesting. Following a study of the Lambs' Tale of the Merchant of Venice I read about the Duck of Venice who presided at the trial of Antonio, of how

Bassanio bought a high-powered car to visit Portia and how finally it was 'his noble ability and his high breath (for 'birth') that overpowered Portia to love him'. In addition I had to continue with my study of Chinese. In 1941 my syllabus included newspaper Chinese, Sun Yatsen's *The Three People's Principles* and the whole New Testament (I had previously been assigned selected parts only) both in the 'National Language' and in Cantonese. I learnt a lot more from the staff who enabled me to 'earth' the academic with life around me.

After the Japanese occupation of Hong Kong the two Wa Ying Schools were disbanded, filtered through the Japanese lines to the North of the province which still remained in Free China and regrouped as a co-educational school at Shiukwaan on the North River, later to be renamed Kukong and once again in the 1980s resuming the name of Shiukwaan (Shaoguan). Shiukwaan was actually taken by the Japanese early in 1945 but at the end of the war (in August) many of the masters and boys sailed happily down the North River to Canton and Fatshan (Foshan) glad to be back in their old home. More of Shiukwaan later in my story but let me mention something that warmed my heart. In 1983 a lady from Cromer was on a package tour to China. She found herself in Canton on a Sunday morning and attended one of the churches that had been re-opened. The minister welcomed her and discovered that she had met me recently. He asked her to pass on his warm greetings and explained that as a boy he had been to Wa Ying School in Hong Kong. It must have been something like forty-three years since I had taught him!

4 · The Eighteen-Day War

So to Pearl Harbour and all that – 8 December 1941 for us, but 7 December for history books because Pearl Harbour is the other side of the Pacific date line. As early as July 1940 the Chairman, Donald Childe, sent me up to Canton to order all wives and children, and to advise single women workers to leave at once for

Hong Kong and evacuation. I failed in my mission only in the case of Dorothy Purry, a senior colleague who had come out for evangelistic work in Canton as long before as 1913. She went to bed quietly but in the morning confessed to me what a serious thing it was not to take the Chairman's advice explaining that she had prayed about it very carefully during the night and was sure that it was God's will that she should stay in Canton. In other words she was not budging. I am very sure, though, that there were at the time some cheers in heaven where she now is. I do not know the circumstances of another senior woman worker, this time a teacher, Sadie Laird from the Irish Methodist Church, but I know that she was later reported missing, presumably dead, and she was able to read her own obituary in the *Methodist Recorder*. She said she found it most interesting.

People generally were beginning to realize that the Japanese were preparing to attack Hong Kong. Now in 1941 they moved more troops to the border. By way of response the British sent the two Indian Regiments to the New Territories hills for manoeuvres. The Royal Scots were already in the New Territories and I often travelled back to Shatin from Kowloon on the train with some of them, who always seemed to have imbibed generous amounts of alcohol. I remember thinking, 'God help the Japs if these chaps are ever let loose on them.' I was reflecting the general attitude of the Europeans in Hong Kong. We were sure that the Japanese could not take the colony. How foolish we were! In the event the Japanese army attacked with vastly superior numbers (80,000 men was one figure given) – we expected this – but in their rubber-soled canvas boots they ran rings round our men both in the New Territories and later on Hong Kong island. Apart from the Indian Regiments our men were burdened with full kit and trained more for a European war with dependence on roads and motorized transport.

I well remember the first warning we had at the school that war was upon us. I was in the village and noticed a man who might well have been a Japanese taking photographs in an entirely open way. I phoned the police sergeant at our local police station. He was sitting at the end of the telephone and replied, 'There is nothing I can do. My men are all at their emergency stations. I am alone.' A lonely vigil indeed and a frightening one! The Senior School's own contribution to preparation had been a few days before when we sent a small party of teachers and senior boys to reconnoitre a path through the rice-fields and over the Kowloon hills to the Junior School in case means of transport were cut off. It proved a wise move.

Early in the morning of 8 December (our time) the Japanese attacked on all fronts from Pearl Harbour in the far east to Malaysia and Singapore in the west. Just after 8.00 a.m. Japanese planes passed over us and we heard their bombs as they exploded on Kai Tak airfield where there were still three RAF planes. We took our cue. The cross-country route to Kowloon was taken by the whole school, each of us carrying what we could. Later that morning we heard that the road was still open and were able to hire two lorries to return to the school to rescue what property, books, food we could, including my two young dogs. All this, of course, was a great help to the school in its crowded quarters. That night the masters began 'the burning of the books' – all books, magazines, newspapers that might have anything derogatory to say about the Japanese. I had never realized before how difficult it is to burn books and magazines. It took a long time indeed and from time to time I was foolishly assuring them that Hong Kong would never be taken. They wisely and kindly refrained from comment and carried on. After all they had been through all this before in Canton and Fatshan.

The next day I took the ferry across the harbour and like many other missionaries offered my services to the Medical Department. The ferries were stopped later that day by order of the Government and no traffic was allowed across the harbour. I was very effectively cut off from the school where in any case I could have been of little help and indeed a very real embarrassment. Certainly on the 8th, and I think also on this day, I was astounded to meet people who still thought the bombing of the airfield had been part of a manoeuvre arranged by the RAF! I was stationed at the Queen Mary Hospital, the large government hospital on the west side of the island, and put on transport. Jack Johnston, a New Zealand Presbyterian minister, was to work with me. I had a Chinese driver and later on a Welshman and an American and possibly others who were used to lorries. Our task was varied but boiled down to calling at all first-aid posts and relief hospitals in and around the city, discovering their needs and then returning in the afternoon with the goods they required. It sounded straight-forward but was not always easy in the execution; for example, where could these goods be found by comparative strangers? We also had bombing to face in the early days and later mortar fire when the Japanese were on the island. There was also the problem of money. The banks were closed and we were given no cash. We got round this one by offering merchants and factories bits of paper on which I credited the seller with the agreed amount and signed on behalf of the Medical Department of the Hong Kong Government. It worked excellently. The Chinese shopkeepers and merchants were afraid of looting and gladly accepted the bit of paper. After the war I checked with the Medical Department and was assured that every bit of paper I had signed was honoured and the seller paid in full. This said a lot indeed both for the faith of the Chinese and the good name of the Hong Kong Government.

On one occasion I was sent to get a lorryload of rice. Somebody mentioned a 'go-down' (warehouse) on the waterfront and sure enough I found there a mountain of bulging rice bags with a British Fire Brigade Officer sitting all alone on top with a badly sprained ankle and holding a revolver. He was successfully keeping looters away and at the same time giving directions to us and other *bona fide* customers. He wisely insisted that no two lorries should be close together in case this drew the fire of the Japanese. A look across the harbour emphasized the incredible situation we were in for modern warfare. We could see units of the Japanese army the other side of the harbour and no doubt they had binoculars trained on us. This Fire Brigade Officer later turned up in the Civilian Internment Camp and I remember him as one of so many unsung heroes in this extraordinary war.

Another assignment raised a tricky ethical problem. A number of the first-aid posts were running short of batteries for their torches. There had been a run on the shops and I could not find a battery anywhere. By chance I bumped into a couple of beach-combers – English, I regret to say – who were wandering about the colony in an ancient car and serving their own ends. They promised to take me to a torch and battery factory if I would give them a quarter of all the batteries I acquired. So I signed for four wooden boxes and gave them one. I still think that under the circumstances I was right.

On another occasion we came across a Chinese lying wounded in the gutter. I think that a small shell had wounded him in the legs. We picked him up and delivered him to a nearby hospital which I should say was a private affair and not a Government hospital. The doctor in charge refused to accept him and after a long argument we laid him down at their main door and went our way. It was getting late and we had to finish our rounds. I learnt that day that we could not stop to clear casualties. It was a matter of priorities and in the limited time allowed it was more important to keep the first-aid posts and relief hospitals going. It was a searing decision and hit me still harder later when I learned that Eric Moreton, a colleague of mine, who was one of two English Methodist ministers stationed in Hong Kong, had received a similar wound from a small shell which took off part of his right arm. He was returning from a relief hospital in which he was serving as chaplain. He was left lying at the side of the road and when some merciful soul finally got him to hospital it was too late to save him. One does not forget these things. *C'est la guerre* and only those who have been involved know what a filthy business it is.

A more fortunate incident occurred when we were using an ambulance to take relief nurses to the other side of the city. We had to drive along the only road that ran by the side of the Naval Dockyard and linked the two parts of the city. The methodical Japanese used to start shelling from the other side of the harbour at 8.00 a.m. precisely and I think it was 5.00 or 5.30 when they stopped. Whether we were a little late or whether they were not playing the game I do not know, but again it was a small shell that hit the road ahead of us. We were going at a good pace. It made a hole in the road, blackened the front of the ambulance, but did not even break the windscreen. We were all startled to say the least but no one was hurt.

The surrender of Hong Kong was inevitable. Hope still

flickered in European breasts. Persistent rumours came through that the Chinese army was advancing to relieve us and an official bulletin was quoted in a local one-page newspaper to this effect. Nobody seemed to reflect that as the Chinese army had been unable to hold Canton it was hardly likely that it would be in a position to save Hong Kong. We had no support from the air or the sea. The few small and out-of-date RAF planes had been destroyed at the outset and the few naval vessels had got away by the skin of their teeth. These included an MTB on which a newspaper correspondent was lucky enough to escape. The Japanese air force had nearby airfields and some of their navy had gathered for the kill. The Colony had some mighty guns in massive emplacements but they were designed to defend the colony against an attack from the sea and were facing the wrong way. Some guns of size must have been able to face the other way for we were sure that it was our guns that we heard pounding away at regular intervals during the first few nights. Tragically only a week or so before the Japanese attack 2,000 Canadian troops, the Winnipeg Grenadiers and the Royal Rifles of Canada, arrived to strengthen the garrison. They were not regular troops and many looked as though they had been tall and tough farmers in civilian life. I had to bury a number later on, a heavy task indeed, and they belonged to the Winnipeg Grenadiers. They knew nothing about the geography of the island and it was said that much of their equipment had not arrived. We heard that they fought well but they never had a chance to acclimatize themselves or to fit in. The Middlesex Regiment and the Hong Kong Volunteer Defence Force completed our tally of fighting men. Our misery was deepened by the news on the radio that the 'Prince of Wales' and the 'Repulse' had been sunk off the Malayan coast on 10 December. By 12 December the Japanese had full control of Kowloon on the other side of the harbour. By evening on 13 December the British forces had all been evacuated to Hong Kong proper. The siege of the island had begun.

On the 14th and again on the 17 December the Japanese sent a motor launch across the harbour under a white flag. They called upon the new Governor, who had only arrived in the colony a few weeks before, to surrender but the offer was refused. The

Japanese were able to land men at North Point to the east of the main city during the night of the 18th. One of our missionaries, Bert Alton, who was there collecting coal for the Nethersole, the London Missionary Society Hospital, saw them coming in small boats and phoned Army Headquarters but was told he was imagining things. The fighting now continued on this part of the island.

On 17 December I was given an additional job. The Queen Mary Hospital mortuary was filled with dead bodies, first of all from the city but soon also from the Winnipeg Grenadiers, who looked giants beside the Chinese. I was given some coolies from the Emergency Burial Centre and asked to clear the mortuary and keep it clear. This was comparatively easy for the first few days because the roads were clear to a cemetery on the other side of the city, but by 21 December this area was being heavily shelled by the Japanese as they fought their way west. It then became a matter of burying anywhere we could. Amazingly the telephone system continued to work and each evening I would phone the Emergency Burial Centre to tell them how many I had buried and where. On the 22nd the hospital coolies went on strike and I could not blame them. They had a rotten job and worked hard but it had become impossible for us to pay them in any regular way. We were able to pacify them with one lump sum of money and promise of regular issues of rice from the hospital store. Fortunately it was easy digging for them that day as we had permission to use the University Sports Council Ground not far from Queen Mary Hospital. After that we had to follow the road leading to the south of the island. I should explain that basically Hong Kong is a mass of volcanic rock and soil is scarce. We found it deep enough in the grounds of an evacuated Roman Catholic seminary – Bethany, I think it was called. Here we were able to dig a long deep trench. After that we had to pick on small plots, often gardens of evacuated houses. It was somewhere here that I bumped into a Captain Diggens who was in charge of burial arrangements for the army. We had a two-man consultation on the whole problem of burial and then we parted. I was to meet him after the war at Shiukwaan on the North River, a hundred and forty miles north of Canton, where he came on an official visit as I shall later narrate. It was the name that intrigued me and he proved to be efficient and easy to work with, though on this occasion he was overwhelmed as we all were with impossible tasks. One of the saddest sights I saw along this road was a stream of Chinese from the direction of Aberdeen but in particular British and Canadian soldiers completely cut off from their units, wandering along, worn-out and hungry, dirty and dispirited. The Japanese were not far behind, they all said.

We were tired, even those of us with the Queen Mary Hospital as our base. I see in the brief diary that I was able to keep that on 23 December I recorded: 'Today I have been transport man, undertaker, coal-heaver, grave-digger, parson and stretcher-bearer.' The reference to parson included a ten-minute burial service, again on the University Sports Field, with a medical student whose wife had been buried there an hour or two earlier. Two others came with me from the hospital. It was the only occasion in this whole grim task of burial when I had any idea of the identity of the people I was burying and the only occasion when a relative or other mourners could be present.

Christmas Day was a day never to be forgotten. For some days we had been expecting Japanese troops to arrive at the hospital. While we could see the situation for ourselves in our trips to the city, we had only the wildest rumours to guide us as to what was happening on the south side of the island. A Mr Anslow was in charge of all hospital stores and I had been assisting him in my spare moments. I must admit that I was a little taken aback when he told me that he was about to issue chastity belts to the nurses. He explained however that he would not be requiring my help as he felt that as a married man it was a matter for him to deal with personally. I remember feeling a little relieved at the time (how did they work, anyhow?), although afterwards I regretted missing the opportunity of seeing him doing his best to explain everything to the nursing staff. I have often wondered since how many hospitals in the United Kingdom carry chastity belts in their store-rooms. Today, however, was Christmas Day, another working day. At 6.30 a.m. I went down to check that they were getting a lorry ready, after which I took part in a service of Holy Communion. About 7.25 two of us went to visit some of the more

27

accessible First Aid Posts. Bombing had again been heavy in some parts of the city. We returned for some breakfast and prepared for grave-digging. A Christmas dinner with plum pudding was nobly provided by the kitchen staff. And then came the end. About 4.00 p.m., having been in the Bacteriological Institute for plasma, I fortunately called in at the Ellis Kadourie First Aid Post just as a telephone message came through to say that we had surrendered. I had to help the First Aid Post evacuate with all speed to Kings College and then return hurriedly to Queen Mary Hospital. On the way we saw white sheets hanging up all around us. It was incredible how quickly the news had spread. I have never been clear exactly where the pit of the stomach is situated but that is where all my feeling was concentrated then. Back in the hospital, all we could do was to wait. We switched on the radio. The good old BBC Overseas Service was functioning. We were invited to join them for a Christmas Day party at the Overseas Club in London. The news assured us that the stubborn and heroic defence of Hong Kong was continuing!

We surrendered unconditionally. We were beaten hands down. In the weeks that followed many civilians found it hard to come to terms with what had happened. They were scared, they were angry, they were bitter, they were ashamed, they felt terribly let down by our own side, they questioned the wisdom of defending Hong Kong at all. It was understandable and indeed this bitterness could be explained, even in part justified, if one so wished. But who was there who understood each facet of a most complicated situation and in a position to judge? The bitterness subsided as we had to face the realities of the present even though it never disappeared in the minds of many. In the same way there was bitterness towards the army, again with some justification, but not by those who had seen the actual conditions on the island. So far as I know the evacuation from the mainland was carried out hurriedly but in good order. It was on the island that order gave way to chaos (to what extent I do not know) as once again the lightly-armed Japanese soldiers, silent in rubber-soled shoes, ran rings round our men. I suspect that control from the centre became impossible and that it became impossible to keep the Army Headquarters informed as to what was happening on the ever-changing and mobile battle areas. Let us hope that all bitterness has evaporated over the years and that compassion only is left. For myself I felt intensely sorry for the army, just as I later felt intense sympathy in the Internment Camp for the wives who lost husbands, for those in particular who were never told for many months whether their husbands were alive or dead, for mothers with young children who had to face nearly four years of starvation and overcrowding. Let the cold print of history books and recent television films describe it as they will, it will never be understood; it had to be experienced.

5 · Banzai

At some point I must say something about the Japanese atrocities. Let me say it now. A more detailed account which includes individual statements by eye-witnesses is given by John Stericker in his book, *A Tear for the Dragon*, published by Arthur Barker in 1958. Suffice it to say that when we moved into the Civilian Internment Camp on Stanley Peninsular our accommodation included St Stephen's College, the Hall of which had been used as an emergency hospital. When the Japanese soldiers arrived in the morning of Christmas Day the two doctors in charge went to meet them and were promptly shot. Many of the patients, most of them wounded in the fighting, were either shot or bayoneted. Because it is not enough to refer to these things in general terms let me give part of one of the statements referred to above. It comes from one of the nurses present at the time:

> Five of the nurses were put into a room with some Chinese women. The latter were first removed and outraged, returning to the room when the Japanese had finished with them. The three younger of the five English nurses were then removed, and never again seen alive. The other two nurses were taken to a room on the other side of the building. Here they were hurled on to some mattresses and left for the night. There was blood

everywhere and sandwiched between the mattresses were the bodies of Chinese women, some of whom were wearing the St John's Ambulance badge. At daybreak the remaining nurses were told to go and dress the surviving wounded.

The nurses found the bodies of Colonel Black and Captain Whitney. A number of the bodies of shot or bayoneted wounded were lying around the rooms and corridors. A padre and a nurse found the bodies of three murdered and outraged English girls piled on top of one another outside the door on the east side of the building.

The Stanley affair was a particularly appalling incident. At the War Crime Courts in Hong Kong after the war an excuse was offered that the Japanese officers lost control of their men. Be that as it may, looting, rape, torture, cold-blooded murder and mindless destruction occurred in many places – to what extent I do not know but it was directed at Chinese as well as foreigners. One of the many rumours that went round was that there has been a kind of black tradition down the centuries that when troops capture a city they are allowed to do what they like for twenty-four hours. This may be doubted as it stands but there seemed to be no control of the rank and file for some such period. Perhaps this is but one facet of a broader problem. There were many signs that the Japanese army did not have the expertise either in trained men or in prepared plans to take over a city or island such as Hong Kong. In the first few weeks it seemed as if they were playing it all by ear and learning as they went along. There was great confusion and much unnecessary suffering. Many of us too could not forget the atrocities that were recorded when the Japanese took Nanking in the war against China.

Having said all this it was remarkable how quickly much of the normal life of the city revived. People began to walk in the streets again. A few teahouses opened. Long lines of hawkers appeared in the streets selling whatever they could lay their hands on, which was mostly loot. Many shops opened in the New Year with such goods as they had managed to retain. It was always risky for 'foreigners' but many began to go out and found themselves unwittingly backing a new kind of trade. Japanese soldiers would politely ask the time and, if the victim was able, equally politely, to tell him, the watch would be confiscated. Fountain pens (no ball-points then) tended to go the same way. Before petrol began to get scarce many Japanese soldiers had joy rides in 'borrowed' cars left undamaged in the roads during the fighting. One such amateur driver drove up to the Queen Mary Hospital which involved a winding road climbing steeply round two hairpin bends. It was a small van and he drove it over the edge at the top. It somersaulted three times and ended right side up on the lowest stretch. We watched fascinated. The door opened and the soldier came out, rubbed his head and walked off apparently unscathed apart from bruises.

At the Queen Mary Hospital life continued as near normal as possible. We began to run short of food and oil (for the boilers). Even before the surrender we were one day told by the Hospital Superintendent to expect the Japanese that afternoon. In the event nobody bothered with us until the day after the surrender when some Japanese plus horses occupied the European staff flats and some of the Chinese doctor's quarters but to our relief left us alone. Nothing further happened until 12 January when a guard of fifty-one Japanese was billeted in the remaining doctors' flats. Due preparations were therefore made in good time. All alcoholic drink (and there was a lot, mainly in private ownership, in the Quarters) was collected and poured down sinks. A sad sight for many but all knew that Japanese soldiers were infinitely more dangerous when drunk. I found myself in another 'burning of the books' but this time we had a hospital incinerator to help.

Amazingly our outside work carried on as there was no one else to take our place. On 26 December my grave-diggers failed to turn up. Two of us had the very unpleasant task of burying five Canadians who had been blown up by a hand-grenade tossed into a pill-box. So far as possible we still visited the relief hospitals and met as many of their needs as possible. We made armbands from hospital bandages, sewed on Red Crosses and travelled in an ambulance. I remember learning two important Japanese words which are firmly inscribed in my mind to this day. 'Buin Ikimas' is how I wrote them and it meant, 'I am going to the hospital.' We had little trouble. A bow and politeness seemed to help and we hoped that they imagined that we were high-ups in the Colony's Medical Service. Actually after four days (on 29 December) we were given an official permit for petrol for the ambulances, dead carts and dustcarts. This gave us considerable standing. It was due, like so much else that was done for us now and later in the Internment Camp, to the Director of Medical Services, Dr Selwyn-Clarke (later to be Governor of the Seychelles Islands). The Japanese had very wisely allowed him to carry on as Director. I don't think they gave him any special authority but they evidently had a high regard for him. He moved to the French Hospital to the east of the city which was neutral ground and reckoned to belong to Vichy France. He operated from there with one or two drivers and trucks and more will be said later of what they were able to do when the Civilian Internment Camp at Stanley came into being.

On Sunday 28 December I had an unusual expedition with him. He was anxious about two ANSs (Auxiliary Nursing Sisters) who had last been heard of at Lyemun Barracks, occupied at first by British troops and now by the Japanese. They were missing and he hoped to find them. He wanted some kind of interpreter. He knew of no one who spoke Japanese but it was thought that the Japanese had been so long in South China that they must have picked up something of Cantonese Chinese and for want of a better the lot fell on me. We set out along the main coast road of the city and had no trouble with sentries. The Japanese were worried about the water supply which had been damaged in the bombing (the main supply came from the mainland under the harbour) and they had given him an official sticker for his car windscreen authorizing him to have free passage in and about the city in order to get the supply going again. We approached Lyemun Barracks to the east of the city. These were built on a hill and it occurred to him that it might look a little suspicious to seek entry in connexion with the water supply. We could see a number of bodies of British soldiers whom the Japanese had not bothered to bury and so he changed his tack. We were now going as representing the Medical Services Department to find out how many bodies there were and to give them burial. The sentries on duty were not at all inclined to let us in. This is where my

Cantonese was supposed to help. I tried to explain that we were concerned with the dead bodies but it was hard going. It seemed that the Japanese soldiers had picked up their Cantonese in a rather different walk of life from my own. I could not remember the word for 'bury'. The officer in charge seemed to think that a statement that the corpses were dead made a daft kind of conversation piece and was beginning to look annoyed. Thanks to descriptive gestures that we were both making, the officer suddenly understood what we had come to do. We were welcome. We explored every inch of the barracks, making a note of the bodies we found and walking round every building at the same time talking loudly in English. We hoped that the ANSs would hear us and be able to shout something in reply if they were there. We drew a blank but we had the satisfaction of knowing that the bodies were later that day properly buried as we had promised. A few days later we heard that the two nurses had made their way across the island to Repulse Bay unharmed and came into the Civilian Internment Camp with the others who had taken refuge in the Repulse Bay Hotel, but not without further adventures.

Finally the Japanese had made all arrangements for a great Victory March through the city. As impressive an array of men and vehicles as they could muster wound its way along the main road along the waterfront. I don't know of any 'foreigner' who saw it but planes flew overhead dropping leaflets and we later gathered that Japanese flags were issued free all along the route for bystanders to wave. The Japanese press was there. It was a day of triumph and celebration for the Japanese. 'Banzai' was the cry – 'Ten Thousand Years' for the Japanese New Order in East Asia. There was not a large turnout of the Chinese populace. They thought their own thoughts and reckoned that ten thousand years was going it a bit and that two or three years might see them off. They were much nearer the truth.

6 · The Civilian Internment Camp at Stanley

(Or, to quote its original designation, as translated by the Japanese into English, 'The Foreigners Internists Quarters of the Foreign Division of Political in charge Department of the Great Nippon Military Head Quarter Civil Government'. Regulations followed but were soon found to be as impossible as the title.)

Early in January the Japanese attempted to deal with a very urgent problem affecting British, Americans and Europeans who had by now exhausted any cash they may have had. The Banks were all closed and many people had lost their homes. Notices went up in the evening of 4 January that all American, British and Dutch subjects were to assemble the next day at 9.30 a.m. on the Murray Parade Ground. Some 1,500 men, women, children and babies turned up and were herded together under terrible conditions in cheap Chinese hotels and brothels. Sanitation was appalling. In one hotel, for example, there were two filthy toilets for a hundred and fifty people. They were pushed into cubicles irrespective of sex. Many of the rooms had no windows and there was no electricity. Each cubicle was six feet by eight feet with a bed that had to do as a seat for four people. The managers of the hotels took advantage of the few who had any money left to sell buns etc. at extortionate prices. The majority had to wait forty-eight hours before any food was offered by the Japanese and they were to stay under these conditions for sixteen days and nights guarded by renegade Indian soldiers with rifles and fixed bayonets. In the end, on 21 January, they were marched off to the waterfront and taken to Stanley on the other side of the island by boat. Others who lived on the Peak or at the University or other outlying areas made their own way to Stanley or were picked up by the Japanese.

At the Queen Mary Hospital we were left very much on our

own until the 21 January when we were taken direct to Stanley by bus. We were told that we could take a suitcase with us but no more. I was given a suitcase by a kind person at the hospital and like many others I was able to take a couple of blankets with me as well. We were amazed to learn that the Americans had been let into the camp with a great deal more luggage than would fill a suitcase! They had brought with them the library (or much of it) from the American Club and a number of fridges. All this was put to communal use in the Camp when the Americans were repatriated in June, the fridges being put in the care of the hospital and the doctors.

I should explain that Stanley peninsula is on the south side of the island. The camp was on the narrow strip of land between Stanley village at one end and barracks at the extreme end. It consisted of St Stephen's Boys' School with the Prep School and five scattered staff bungalows, blocks of flats built for the European Prison Warders, and the Indian Quarters which were built around an open piece of ground, not unlike a village green. A separate block which had served as the Indian Warders' hospital looked east across Tweed Bay and was used as our hospital, the top (second floor) serving as accommodation for the nurses (all, I think, SRNs). The prison itself was outside the camp south of the European Prison Warders' flats. The whole compound was surrounded by barbed wire and guarded first by Chinese, then by Indians, and later at the beginning of 1944 by Formosans. The site was healthy and cool in the summer and was an important factor in our survival. The choice was largely due to the insistence of Dr Selwyn-Clarke.

We also had a small cemetery within the camp on the south-west side not far from the prison. It was set with trees and was to prove a haven of peace for the living as well as the dead. We found the graves of some of the earliest settlers in the colony who had died almost exactly a hundred years before. We were to make our own contribution although, at the end of the war, it was found, surprisingly, that our death rate had been no more or not much more than that of an ordinary English city with its additional hazards of accidents, pollution and over-feeding! When an advance group was sent into camp to bury the dead they found that all relics of the atrocities in St Stephen's relief hospital had been burned, including the bodies of those killed. Their remains were buried in the cemetery by our own folk. From time to time we had to bury those of our own number who died. We had to construct a communal coffin so designed that it could easily be retrieved after the burial, but all were buried with respect and love and with a traditional burial service. All were buried in ground that was indeed historic.

Altogether some 2,500 people were crowded into the camp accommodation, most arriving in the last ten days or so of January. An advance group had been told to prepare the place for the rest of the internees but were given no equipment except a few spades and there was little they could do except remove rubbish and debris. They did, however, name and number all the accommodation that was available so that it was possible in the end to register who was living where. The result was that when the internees arrived everything was up for grabs. To a limited degree individuals made way for mothers and children but it was chaos for some days. In the end the Japanese and our own incipient 'government' plus a little public pressure evened out the accommodation, but it was not easy. A married couple, for example, would lay claim to a room and occupy it for several days and would have to be compelled to give it up for a family. Generally speaking all rooms were occupied by as many people as the floor space could contain camp beds or mattresses with minimum space to move about.

So far as I was concerned, I teamed up with Jack Johnston who had been with me at the Queen Mary Hospital. The first evening we parked ourselves in a room in the main European Warders' blocks complete with camp beds. Before night, however, we had to move out to make room for two families with children and in all decency left our camp beds behind us. It had to be a corridor floor that night. The following night Harold Smyth (the Cheung Chau Country dancing master) and I were unable to better the stone floor of the St Stephen's Prep School. I had kept clear of the hospital staff as I felt I had little else to contribute but I then had an invitation to join them to help Mr Anslow with the stores and do odd jobs as they came along. Thus it came about that I joined the men doctors and others at the Leprosarium a couple of hundred yards up the hill behind the hospital and there I was to spend most of the rest of my time in internment.

Since this was my new home let me describe it. It was a fairly new building with one main ward or dormitory plus kitchen, toilet and store room. On its open side it had a small exercise yard which was fenced in by barbed wire and railings with a single lockable gate. Beyond the fence was a grassy bank facing the sea. The building had been built as an isolation block for prisoners who were found to have leprosy. We scrubbed and cleaned it with all the energy we could muster and settled in. We were an interesting mess of eighteen men. There were most of the Government doctors in camp and a number were at the head of their own department. There was the senior Professor in Surgery, the head of the Bacteriological Institute, an X-ray specialist and a VD man who was wondering whether his job would continue after the war in view of the new antibiotics that we were hearing about. There was a Presbyterian ex-missionary doctor, then in private practice in Hong Kong, and another doctor from a New Zealand Presbyterian hospital north of Canton. There was Geoffrey Herklots from Hong Kong University whose chair was either botany or biology (he was expert in both). He had the invaluable faculty of keeping cheerful under all circumstances and spent hours of his time drawing birds and plants to be found inside the camp (many later to be published). For some months (far too many in the opinion of the rest of us) he kept a bamboo snake in a biscuit tin with a glass front beside his bed. It was poisonous and was known to kill children but he assured us that it was unlikely to kill us and in any case it would not bite us unless we trod on it! I must also mention that by way of preparation for the war the Hong Kong Government had employed him to make 'siege biscuits' which were rich in vitamins and other desirable substances and had been stored in hundreds and probably thousands of sealed tins. A few once found their way into our camp as rations from the Japanese. Whether the Japanese army took to them and so accounted for the bulk we never discovered. Last, but not least, he produced a daily supply of vitamin B solution for the duration of camp. The Japanese allowed him a small ration of flour and from some source he secured hops (probably tinned). With the bottled hops and scalded flour he made a starter which took forty-eight hours to mature. This was added to more boiling water and scalded flour and made a yeast within twenty-four hours. Potatoes were used when flour was not available. Up to a hundred people were given a dose each day on a doctor's prescription and this unappetizing mixture must have saved many lives. The 'factory' was a stranded ambulance damaged beyond repair in the war and to which only Herklots had the key.

Let me complete the number of our mess. Two senior engineers from the Taikoo Dockyard had their own valuable contribution to make. Then there was a Sanitation Inspector with whom I worked from time to time and from whom I learnt many interesting facts of life such as the ability of maggots of the common house fly to make their way through five feet of loose earth to daylight. That has remained in my memory ever since as a symbol of the toughness and tenacity of the young of so many insects and animals on this earth – including man! And finally, two parsons, Jack Johnston mentioned above and myself. We had all things in common including such extra rations and food as we were able to buy from time to time or received from parcels outside including the rare Red Cross parcels which the Japanese finally allowed in.

Still in connection with the Leprosarium I must mention the delightful gramophone concerts that we were able to host on the grassy bank outside the wire. A number of gramophone records (as they were then called) turned up in camp. Most were from the American Library but some had been brought in by individuals. Among the 2,600-odd internees, however, there was only one gramophone – my own. It came in a strange way. I had lent the gramophone to my friend and colleague, Eric Moreton (whose sad death I have mentioned) for use in the Happy Valley Relief Hospital to which he was accredited as chaplain. When the sad story of that hospital ended and the horrible ordeal of the sisters was over, one of them, assuming that the gramophone belonged to him, made up her mind that at all costs she would get it to his widow in camp as a kind of tribute to his memory – and she succeeded when she came in herself. It was a very ordinary mechanical His Master's Voice machine, crude by today's standards, but we were able to use it on the grassy bank and anyone was invited. I can imagine no more helpful setting both for lovers of classical music and for learners such as myself than that grassy bank in the quiet of a sub-tropical evening with the sea in front linking us with lands far away and, it sometimes seemed, with other centuries.

In the early days we were involved in an intriguing lesson in self-government. Chaos, of course, had very quickly to give way to order and discipline. Each Block had its own committee which was appointed by popular vote and elected its own 'Blockhead', hardly an honorific title but one which lasted until the last days of the camp. As for the camp as a whole, a 'General Election' was held to appoint a British Communal Council (the American and the Dutch looked after themselves). Those appointed were on the whole the heads of some of the large Hong Kong and International Companies. Two, however, were parsons (Bert Alton and J. E. Sandbach of the Methodist Church) and Mr Ben Wiley of the *South China Morning Post* was Chairman. It was then realized that the only Government official was the Commissioner of Police who had been elected by his own men. Behind this lay a strong anti-government feeling on the part of many of the internees. There were a number of reasons for it but two stood out. Many felt deeply bitter that it had proved hopeless to try to defend Hong Kong and many lives had been lost in the attempt. They felt let down. The second reason was that while the wives and children of non-government civilians had been compulsorily evacuated to Australia and New Zealand or elsewhere, too many Government officials had managed to keep their families with them and there were, therefore, many wives and children who should not have been there. This may sound niggardly, especially when the husbands of evacuated families were glad that their families were away from it all, but it was a fact of camp life at that time. In the crowded condition of the buildings the adults not unnaturally got irritatingly on top of each other very often. As I have already mentioned, each room would contain as many persons as it could contain camp beds (eight persons was by no means unusual) with very limited space to move about. The strain was often greater when a mother with perhaps a child or two was included.

The Communal Council lasted for only a short time and was mainly concerned with the internal administration of the camp. To some extent, however, it also had to deal with the local Japanese. We lacked official Government leaders. Sir Mark Young, the Governor of Hong Kong, who had only been in the colony a few weeks, elected to wear his military hat and had been sent to a Prisoner-of-War Camp in Manchuria. Mr Franklin Gimson (later Sir Franklin), who was the newly-appointed Colonial Secretary and who himself had only arrived as the war started, was kept out of the camp as the official to hand over the colony to the Japanese. When he later arrived in camp he announced that the Communal Council was unconstitutional and appointed his own Advisory Council. This consisted mainly of senior Government officials but did include two or three non-Government men. Not unnaturally some feeling was stirred up but it was gradually recognized that all official dealings with the Japanese had to go through the Colonial Secretary. Undoubtedly he had the most difficult and dangerous job of all. The local Block Committees and 'Blockheads' continued. We soon settled to this 'New Deal' which proved final.

Some food was provided for us in the evening of 21 January when so many of us arrived. My diary records 'some rice and a small portion of a fishy mixture and some soya beans for the evening meal'. The next morning it was rice only but after that, so far as I can remember, the Japanese provided rations for two meals a day which we had to collect and cook in communal kitchens on fires stoked by wood which also we had to collect (and saw and chop) from the jetty. More about food later! As far as the number and nationality of the internees went the official figures on 2 February 1942 were: British 2426; Americans 277; Dutch 54; making a total of 2757. Some Norwegian sailors and Belgians joined us later.

Most of the Americans were repatriated at the end of June 1942 in the Asama Maru. The Canadians followed in September 1943 in the Tei-a Maru. As for the remaining internees there were many old and retired people and, of course, a dearth of men of

40

military age. We were fortunate in having some two hundred police with us. There were many mothers and children. As already mentioned, a number of them ought to have joined the evacuation ships to Australia and elsewhere long before hostilities began but there were quite a number of local British Chinese and Eurasians, many with children. In all we represented a wide and interesting cross-section of the colony's life. Because in those days it was usual for 'top people' to be Europeans we had a considerable number of leading figures in Commerce and Business, in the Government, in the Public Works Department, in the Medical Services, in the Education Department and the Schools and Universities and, for that matter, in the churches.

The authorities in charge of the camp (Chinese for a short time and then Japanese) lived in two houses on a small hill in the centre of the camp. The Japanese were at first civilians under the Foreign Affairs Department but later they were army officers. We became 'the Military Internment Camp' in February 1944. The ordinary internees had little to do with the Japanese directly. It was different for the people who were arrested. Thus four attempted to escape and were tortured and imprisoned for two years, coming out alive, however. In October 1943 ten were involved in the discovery of a radio ('wireless') set and accused of sending and receiving messages from outside through a Chinese driver working for the Japanese. Three were sentenced to fifteen years' imprisonment but seven after torture were shot (some said beheaded) on the beach by the jetty where the firewood was landed. John Fraser, the Defence Secretary, who was posthumously awarded the George Cross was also shot or beheaded about this time. Some bankers who had been retained in the city were arrested and some sent to prison (as was Dr Selwyn-Clarke). Sir Vandeleur Grayburn, Chief Manager of the Hong Kong and Shanghai Bank, died of beri-beri in prison and, some months later, his second-in-command, Mr Edmondston, died in prison of starvation. There were other cases of barbaric treatment. Screams of men, and occasionally women, being tortured could sometimes be heard coming from the prison and, on at least one occasion, from the Japanese Headquarters on the hill within our camp. So far as the camp in general was concerned, however, the

41

major count against the Japanese lay along the lines of culpable neglect. We had roll-calls morning and night; we had to bow to them when we met; we were forbidden to position ourselves on a balcony or anywhere from which we could look down at them, and armed sentries surrounded the camp at all times; but on the whole they left us alone.

7 · Short Commons

The most serious example of culpable neglect after the paucity of drugs for the hospital was the starvation ration of food which continued throughout the three years and eight months the camp lasted. It is true that many of the remaining Chinese population of Hong Kong (down to about half a million) suffered starvation too and it is possible that the Japanese troops were sometimes on hard rations, but the Japanese had assumed responsibility for us and were unwilling to repatriate us. The pre-war League of Nations' basic calorie requirement for an adult (eleven-stone) in a temperate climate and not engaged in manual labour was 2,400 calories a day. We were in a sub-tropical climate but all the manual work inside the camp (wood sawing and chopping, cooking, gardening, sanitation etc.) had to be done by internees, mainly the Hong Kong Police and men below the age of retirement. The calorific value of our rations was 1,400 when we entered camp and dropped as the months went by to 1,100. In fact the rations did not reach 2,400 calories until December 1942 and this was due to some bulk Red Cross foodstuffs which the Japanese allowed in and which lasted, with careful use, until March or April the following year. In January 1945 the average daily intake of calories through the rations sank to 1,300 per day!

The younger men and women did best as they were able to adapt themselves to a rice diet earlier. They often came in for extra food that the older people and some younger women passed over to them, such as particularly stinking salt fish and particularly foul 'water spinach'; also fish heads and eyes which many found it difficult to stomach. It was found that those who had a job of work (not necessarily manual) kept fitter than those who had nothing to do. An interesting feature was the number of elderly folk who withdrew from much of the ordinary life of the community and spent hours each day playing bridge. Young children were often sent milk in the rations and seemed to do reasonably well. Children over the age of eight and especially teenagers suffered most and have probably been suffering in one way or other since, for example with their teeth, to mention only a minor ill.

The hospital was full most of the time. Later in the history of the camp it became too small for our needs and the Leprosarium (described above) was turned into a Sanatorium for twelve TB patients, some five of whom had TB before coming into camp. Our mess, of course, was broken up and we had to find berths elsewhere. There was a steady turnover in dysentery and malaria, several diphtheria cases at Christmas 1942, a few typhus cases and, I think, typhoid. A detailed report of the health of the internees was published in medical journals after the war by Dr Dean Smith who kept careful statistics throughout.

By March 1944 it was proving to be beyond the strength of manual workers to get the work done and five grades of rations were introduced in consultation with the Japanese:

(a) Children below the age of 5   8.708 ozs ⎫
(b) Children between the ages of 6 and 9 10.885 ozs ⎪ of rice
(c) Adults – 'ordinary ration'   13.062 ozs ⎬ per head,
(d) Adults – light workers   17.418 ozs ⎪ per day
(e) Adults – heavy workers   21.770 ozs ⎭

This was the scale on 11 March 1944. Other items of food that came in, e.g. soya beans, sugar, salt, tea, curry, and oil, also fish and vegetables, were rationed in the same proportion. They were not generous! Figures for the first six of these items ranged over one period from 0.213; 0.417; 0.131; 0.243; 0.044; 1.112 ozs in grade (a) to 0.283; 1.252; 0.131; 0.243; 0.089; 2.224 ozs in grade (e). We might also be sent meat in the place of fish. Before the introduction of grading this could range from two ounces (20 March 1942) to a high point of 4.92 ozs in January 1943, but this included the bone (and often short measure). We had one memorable period when the electricity supply in Hong Kong broke down and we had whole sides of slightly smelly Australian lamb from a crippled cold store. Both fish and meat ceased in February 1945 and were not resumed until June 1945.

We owed our survival to a number of factors:

1. The climate and, in particular, the fresh air and sunshine of Stanley Peninsula.
2. Extra vegetables, mainly sweet potatoes, wrested from very poor soil (where it could be found) at first by individuals and later, when the gardens were taken over by order of the Japanese, by communal efforts.
3. Our doctors were able to advise us and to make endless experiments in the matter of vitamins and food values. Advice was given (and not always taken) as to what to buy at the Canteen and for a time the Red Cross representatives in the city were able to send in bran and beans on the doctors' request.
4. On one or two occasions supplies of shark liver oil and thiamin were sent into camp. Probably the largest supply of the latter was in the early days of camp when a few of our number were sheltering in the neutrality of the French hospital and had transport. A member of the Friends' Ambulance Unit in South West China who had been caught in Hong Kong made friends with Japanese soldiers in the Japanese Army Head-quarters (the Hong Kong and Shanghai Bank). He made a point of calling often and was able to locate some large glass containers of vitamin B in liquid form which he had been told about by the medical people. He offered to get rid of these containers which the soldiers only recognized as a nuisance and his offer was accepted. They were loaded in his van and he managed to get them safely into camp. These, and other such supplies, were of course in the control of the doctors, who prescribed them for the most needy cases.
5. A Canteen was opened during 1942 where we could buy extras, usually twice a month. Peanuts, bran, salt, oil, lard, margarine, wong tong (local sugar), egg yolk powder, soya

44

beans and soya bean flour, jam, shaving sticks, tooth powder and toilet paper were all on sale at different times but we were limited to a certain quota and commodities dried up and increased in price as time went on. But we could only buy if we had money!

6. Many were fortunate in having parcels sent in, especially in the early days, by friends in town. My faithful servant, a Chinese 'amah', sent my best suit in (bless her!) but the jacket got lost *en route*. I managed to survive the camp in what I was wearing when I went into camp plus a sun-hat and a pair of trousers made by missionary friends in camp, one of whom had brought in a sewing machine. I kept my brown leather shoes going by learning a cobbler's stitch from a craftsman.

Often the parcels contained food. Our own Missionary Society was able at one time to get a series of food parcels sent in to us from China through Shanghai. They came from a missionary (Swiss or German, I think) called Etling. It was a joy to me after the war when I was passing through Changsha in Hunan province to bump into him. The name rang a bell and I was able to thank him on behalf of us all.

7. Red Cross parcels reached us on three occasions:

2 November 1942, together with some food in bulk, some clothes and some drugs

14 September 1944 – three parcels each

4 March 1945 – just over one parcel each but these appeared to be old food parcels from the previous consignment.

Small amounts of money came in to us in unexpected ways. At the end of 1942 the Shanghai British Residents' Association most kindly and generously sent us enough for a few dollars each. In February 1943 an allowance from the British Government got through. A large part of this was quite rightly kept back for communal use in the purchase of beans, bran and welfare goods through the Red Cross representative in Hong Kong but in February we each received 15 Yen for individual purchases and after that 20 or 25 Yen for several months. The Japanese insisted on separate negotiations for each monthly block grant and this led to delays. As food prices rose, grants to individuals were reduced and then ceased. Grants for bulk buying ceased at a later date.

Many internees could still raise money from about their persons by selling on the black market watches, fountain pens and rings to the Formosan guards through internees who acted as local agents. A gold digger's paradise opened before some internees when it was realized that the Formosans were interested in gold fillings from teeth. The two dentists in camp were kept busy filling in the gaps. Cigarettes became a currency in themselves both for fining our own internees guilty of misdemeanours (the only sanction that the Japanese permitted the Camp Council, the major sanction being public opinion) and for raising money by selling to the moneyed internees.

The black market had in fact created something quite new in camp – a new elite, a moneyed and privileged class consisting of a very small group of middlemen. Gold, etc., went out and food, cigarettes, bread or other requirements came in. In as much as it seemed to be doing down our captors it was held to be reasonably respectable but great care had to be exercised by those engaged in the trade. Agents, if caught, would have been in danger of their lives; the same applied to the Formosan guards involved. The Japanese had to be seen to suppress the trade while at the same time some were getting a rake-off. Black market prices became astronomical during the last year or more. A good watch would sell for Yen 5,000; cigarettes could be bought for anything up to Y50 per packet of ten; at one time bread was coming over the wire (some thought through a drain) at Y120 per catty (1⅓ lbs); bacon and pork costing Y120 per catty went up to Y580 in January 1945 and later still reached Y1,000; on 19 June 1945 peanuts were Y300 per lb; duck eggs were obtainable at Y25–Y35 each; wong tong (local slab sugar) was Y140 in January 1945 and went up to over Y1,000 before the end. Often the trade was in sterling cheques and IOUs' to be honoured after the war.

By way of contrast to the black market, the letters from outside were food of a different kind and helped to keep up our morale. It took many months to arrange an exchange of letters with Great Britain and other countries through the Red Cross. The first main batch of letters from England arrived in March 1943. They were

46

posted in July 1942 and the postmark had the striking injunction, 'Post early in the day'. In May 1943 we were allowed to write a two-hundred-word letter but I think that we were allowed to write short messages on postcards earlier than this. Later we were allowed to write Prisoners-of-War postcards of twenty-five words. Family and friends in England used International Red Cross postcards, also of twenty-five words, which it was hoped would get through the censors more quickly.

8 · Cramped Culture

In numbers we were as many as can be found in a sizeable English village. We lived on top of each other but we had experts in many fields and organized ourselves in ways traditional to a village or a town. A day school was organized from the beginning in the Hall of St Stephen's College, which fortunately was left by the Japanese for our general use. A small hall in what had been the Bowling Club pavilion was also used. The school was divided into Kindergarten, Junior and Senior Departments. The staff included three university professors and four headmistresses and so was of no mean order. Difficulties abounded. We had very few books and little in the way of writing material and for some considerable time all had to sit on the floor. Moreover, all classes had to meet in different parts of one or other of the two halls. We did not produce bookworms but we were able to offer a sound education not only in the three Rs but in coming to terms with the variegated life of the camp and a pretty wide understanding of the world outside and its previous history.

As time went on we ventured into the field of adult education. Shorthand and typing lessons were given and after the war Pitmans issued certificates for exams set in camp. Lectures on a variety of subjects were given over the space of three years and were well attended. On a single evening there might be as many as three or four lectures on offer, some more popular and some more specialized. During the long months when the electricity was cut

47

off and we had no light, lectures were often given on the stairway where the steps offered hard but convenient seats. More spontaneously, discussion groups were arranged and often met in the open air, one favourite place being a small quarry that occupied part of our camp site.

We had in camp a number of engineers and craftsmen who proved invaluable in making cookery utensils and tools of many kinds for our common use. At one time we were having trouble with the rice, which came to us in large sacks. Hungry Chinese in Hong Kong had learnt the art of extracting rice and replacing it with stones so that its weight was unaltered. It was extremely unpleasant to eat and extremely bad for the teeth. Our engineers came up with a Heath Robinson contraption with a series of grids in which you turned a handle and the stones were gathered in one place and the rice in another. All this kind of activity called for skills in carpentry and metalwork. We had a number of teenage boys in camp and the idea arose that they could become apprentices. A special company was floated to train them. We had our own exams, based on standards prevailing outside. I myself taught for a time in the school but later was detailed to coach a likely candidate for Oxford University in Latin. It was certainly good for me as I had to brush up my very rusty Latin. It was good cheer for his several tutors to hear after the war that he had been accepted at Oxford – in spite of my Latin! I never heard the exact details but it was also true that the appropriate outside bodies accepted some of the qualifications of our apprentices after the war was over. The school held two matriculation examinations, one in 1943 and one in 1945, and it was hoped that the successful candidates would be recognized by the London Matriculation Board. Some police sat them as well as children.

The same Hall at St Stephen's also served for church services on Sunday and for the production of plays, ranging from a Nativity Play in 1942 and 1943, John Masefield's 'Good Friday' at Easter 1943, and a Passion Play written and produced by the Rev. Cyril Brown, who had earlier been serving in the Missions to Seamen. Other plays included 'A Midsummer Night's Dream', Noel Coward's 'Private Lives', 'The Housemaster', J. B. Priestley's 'Laburnum Grove' and a stage-rendering of the 'White Cliffs of

Dover'. Two original ballets were produced by a professional teacher of ballet from Shanghai. The YMCA ran a series of Sunday night lectures on a variety of subjects religious, historical, scientific and biographical. These often filled the gallery as well as the body of the Hall. We had the talents and we learnt initiative and improvization as we went.

Special mention must be made of the weekly concerts. They were held on the Bowling Green where there was room for the several hundreds who attended and they were held in the cool of the evening. Happy memories. The compere was Cyril Brown who handled each concert excellently, having been well trained, no doubt, in his dealings with seamen. The items were as varied as you might expect but some of the songs remain clearly in my memory and I am sure in the memories of all present: 'When the nightingale sang in Berkeley Square'; Noel Coward's 'We'll gather lilac in the spring again and walk together down an English lane' and many more. The recitation, 'The White Cliffs of Dover', I have already mentioned. They were nostalgic, if you like, but a healthy boost to morale as were songs we sang about possible repatriation, which never came off for the British, but again hope stiffened our resolve to survive. There were, I am sure, negotiations going on about repatriating us, first of all via the Portuguese Colony of Lourenco Marques and then via Goa. 'Sail away' with the chorus 'Afloat on a boat on the way to Lourenco Marques', and 'We're going to go to Goa on Repatriation Day' became 'Top of the Pops' before there were any Pops. Lourenco Marques and Goa were staging posts for transfer to neutral ships. It was a sad blow when the concerts were stopped. It happened in this way. For propaganda purposes the Japanese sent photographers to take pictures of us all enjoying a concert. As soon as the word got around some members of the audience put up their hands in a Churchillian 'V' for Victory sign. This was taken up by the audience as a whole, along with cheering and clapping. We appeared indeed to be a happy throng. The photographers and the local Japanese were delighted. Unfortunately someone back in Tokyo had heard of the 'V' for Victory sign and there must have been a great fury at the leg-pull. At any rate orders came back that concerts were to cease forthwith.

49

It was, of course, highly dangerous to take the mickey out of a Japanese. We had to bow to them when they inspected the camp, but there were occasions when we found our own way of hitting back. They were particularly sensitive to being called 'Nips' (from Nippon = Japan). So far as we were concerned, Japanese planes were Nip planes and piloted by Nips. Cyril Brown on one occasion raised a barrage of cheering when he introduced a concert with, 'What a delightful evening it is, cool and fresh and not a nip in the air'. The Japanese party from the hill who always attended our concerts looked definitely surprised at the translation which more or less correctly said there was no sign of frost. There is never frost in Hong Kong! In the same way one of the precious gramophone records we had in camp consisted of songs from the Mikado. It gave us an odd quirk of delight to play the first chorus:

> If you want to know who we are,
> We are gentlemen of Japan,

which concludes:

> If you think we are worked by strings,
> Like a Japanese marionette,
> You don't understand these things;
> It is simply Court etiquette.
> Perhaps you suppose this throng
> Can't keep it up all day long?
> If that's your idea, you're wrong, oh!

I have mentioned the American Club Library which the Americans in camp left for us when they were repatriated. It was realized that in fact there were a lot of other books in the camp which internees had brought in with them or which were in the camp buildings already. These were all gathered into three main libraries from which books could be borrowed by any internee. Up to the end of May 1945 we were allowed copies of the English newspaper that the Japanese had started in Hong Kong. It put over heavy Japanese propaganda but by reading between the lines and referring to back numbers we had a pretty good idea of how things were going in Europe. The fighting in the Pacific was in

50

favour of the Japanese for what seemed a very long time but when the tide began to turn they made sure that it favoured them still, almost to the end. After 31 May 1945 no newspapers were allowed into camp.

9 · The Church

I hesitate to give a separate chapter to church affairs because one of the features of the camp was that we were not polarized into church and non-church, religious affairs, parsons and laymen, with various chips on our shoulders (on both sides) as we are in this country. We were all equal in that we were all reduced to the bare necessities of life and all were hoping to survive. For that reason we were all equally interested in any activity that was offered. Church people (including parsons) took at least their fair share of the administrative and manual work of the camp while on the other hand it was at times surprising who came along to church services or to lectures and discussion groups of a definitely religious nature. I treasure the memory, for example, of the lady who came away from the performance of John Masefield's 'Good Friday' and was heard to remark to a friend afterwards, 'It was all very well done but rather sad, don't you think?' From my own point of view the most interesting development in camp was that of church life and so a separate chapter it must be. In those far-off days joint worship with the two hundred or so Roman Catholics was out of the question. They joined in where they could, for example in Masefield's 'Good Friday', but kept to themselves for Mass and worship services under the pastoral care of an American RC priest who nobly stayed behind when the other Americans were repatriated. But on the Protestant side we moved further ecumenically than has yet been possible in this country today except in the growing number of Local Ecumenical Projects.

In camp we had members of twenty-two separate denominations. The main bodies were Anglican, Methodist, Congregational, Presbyterian (including the Church of Scotland), Baptist, the Society of Friends, the Salvation Army and the Roman Catholics. One of the Quakers was William Sewell, a professor of chemistry at Chengtu University, who later wrote a book about our life in camp entitled *Strange Harmony* published by the Edinburgh House Press in 1946. At the very beginning of camp an extempore meeting of ministers and clergy realized that a series of denominational services in St Stephen's Hall throughout Sunday was ridiculous. On the very first Sunday there was a United Communion or Eucharist at 9.00 a.m. with worship services at 11.30 a.m. and 3.30 p.m. On Tuesday 27 January there was an important meeting of British and American clergy at which a Committee was elected and suggestions mooted. The elected Chairman was Frank Short of the Congregational Church, the vice-Chairman Dr Shoop (a senior and wise American missionary); Harry Wittenbach (later to be Secretary of the Church Missionary Society) and myself were joint treasurers and there were six other members. The following Sunday we had a single united service of worship at 12.00. After that we went through a period of experiment about times and types of services but from the very start there was a United Congregation and ministers of more than one denomination took part in each service. Gradually we became more stereotyped. At 9.00 a.m. there was a Communion Service or Eucharist following the Order of a particular denomination. If it was an Anglican Order a Free Church minister would assist and vice-versa. The same was true of the 12.00 (or 11.30) worship service and sermon, the preacher being of a different denomination from the Leader. A similar evening service took place at 6.30.

Later the arrangements were:

8.45 a.m.   Holy Communion according to the Anglican Prayer Book (choral once a month).

9.45 a.m.   Morning Service and Sermon. Alternately Mattins and Free Church. On the first and third Sundays of the month this was followed by a Free Church Order of Holy Communion, Congregational, Presbyterian and Methodist in turn.

3.45 p.m.   Afternoon Service and Sermon, alternately Evensong and Free Church.

52

6.30 p.m.   Short service of praise with address. This would be
more informal and heartier.

Daily Prayers were said in a small room at 8.30 a.m., using
Anglican Morning Prayer on Mondays and Wednesdays with the
Litany on Fridays and a Free Church simpler and freer style on
Tuesdays, Thursdays and Saturdays. Later this changed to
Morning Prayers as follows: on Mondays and Saturdays 'free'
prayer either extempore or read as the Leader wished; on
Tuesdays it would be Mattins; on Wednesdays a Quaker Quiet
Time; on Thursdays Holy Communion and on Fridays Mattins
and the Litany. In April 1942 we had the traumatic experience of
losing a left-wing evangelical group (mainly Americans) who
already were holding their own Open Air Meeting and broke
away from us, forming their own committee. I went to one of
their open air meetings and noted in my diary that I found their
presentation of the gospel very superficial.

A Sunday School was started from the beginning of camp by
two lay Anglican Leaders (Winifred Penny and Charlotte Bird),
trained in modern Sunday School methods. Winifred Penny was
appointed Lay Superintendent and a week or two later I was
appointed Ministerial Superintendent. Fortunately we saw eye to
eye and together with a team of experienced teachers we gradually
worked out a satisfactory system. On my first visit to the Sunday
School in February 1942 I found some thirty-five children and
twenty adults worshipping together with the adults going out to
their own class after the opening (a pattern familiar to older
generations both in England and America). Over the following
weeks and months we were able to establish an Intermediate
Department which met in the afternoon because of lack of space
and a Primary Department which met in the morning. Later
still we started a Senior Department which developed into a
Junior Church. This met on Sunday mornings before church. A
Teachers' Training Class met each week.

The adults were catered for by quite separate Bible Classes and
Discussion Groups. Ward Services and Communion Services
were regularly held in the hospital. We had an interesting
problem with the wine. Because of the fear of infection, especially
TB, common cups (chalices) were out of the question (as indeed

they already were even in Anglican Churches in China). It was common in China to use individual Chinese wine cups but these were not available. In the end we did what we understood was common in the Church in India, which was to use a spoon to drop the wine into the mouth. This was in the hospital. I cannot remember what we did in the main camp services.

After the Americans were repatriated in June 1942 there were fifteen ministers and clergy left. We met for devotions, business and discussion every Monday afternoon on a verandah. On the administrative side a Lay Council was formed which in its turn produced a Church Fellowship of several scores of people who formed the inner circle of the church. At Christmas and Easter the church came into its own in the life of the whole camp, as it did in particular for the Thanksgiving Service on 17 August 1945 when we were sure our Far Eastern war really was over and when St Stephen's Hall was filled to overflowing. We had Bible Classes and Discussion Groups in plenty, some tackling quite profound problems that would face the nations after the war as well as studies into the nature of man as an individual. *Man against Himself* by someone with a name like Mannheim was a book which I remember had considerable influence. Eddington's *The Philosophy of Physical Science*, Unamuno's *The Tragic Sense of Life*, Nicolas Berdyaev's *The Destiny of Man* were others. We sometimes held open air services and in September 1943 we had an evangelical campaign which we dubbed 'Quo Vadis?' The name came from a book based on the legend that as Peter was escaping from Rome and martyrdom he was met by Christ with his cross going the other way and asking Peter, 'Where are you going?' Peter got the message and returned to Rome where he was crucified. It seemed at the time to have vital overtones for us as individuals, as a community and indeed for mankind as a whole. Daily talks were given based on obstacles that prevented many of the internees from accepting Christ or joining the church. Thus the advertised subjects were Obstacle No. 1, The Bible; Obstacle No. 2, God; Obstacle No. 3, Jesus Christ as Son of God, and so on. In the follow-up people were invited to join a Bible Class and Discussion Groups but also asked to write down any subject which they felt had been ignored or inadequately dealt with.

There was perhaps a link between this campaign and what was very much a spontaneous movement that spread through the camp the following year. I have mentioned above that lecturers had sometimes made use of the many stairways in the camp. In August 1944 the electricity was cut off (no coal left in Hong Kong was what we heard) and as a result there was an acute shortage of water as the pumps were not working. The months that followed were particularly difficult. I think it started on one or two stairways in the Indian Quarters. As dark fell one or two people got the idea of sitting on the stairs, reading a few verses of the Bible, praying and being quiet for a short time. Word got around and 'The Epilogue', as it came to be called, became a feature of many stairways throughout the camp. People would come from their rooms and quietly sit down somewhere on the stairs within earshot of what was going on. It could not have been simpler, and for the most part it could not have been shorter, but it brought a blessing to many, sometimes courage, sometimes reassurance, sometimes a sense of fellowship with loved ones far away and, I am very sure, very often a sense of the presence of God.

A Tribute to the Rev Kiyoshi (John) Watanabe

At this point I cannot move on with my story without paying tribute to John Watanabe, a Lutheran minister who was conscripted into the Japanese army and served as an interpreter for a time in the Prisoners-of-War Camp at Shamshuipo Kowloon and for a time in our own. He won the respect and gratitude of very many people in both camps and in 1960 appeared on one of the early 'This is your Life' television programmes.

He was born into a Buddhist family and became a Christian partly because his older brother, while at college studying medicine, sent him a copy of the Bible and partly because, while he himself was studying at college and seeking for more information about the Christian faith, he was told by his brother to seek out a Lutheran pastor. His family accepted his conversion in a very understanding way and he spent five years in the Lutheran Theological Department of a university before graduating as a Lutheran pastor himself. He was later invited to the Tenth World

Sunday School Convention in Los Angeles and also spent two years at a Theological Seminary at Gettysburg.

He was living in Hiroshima with his family when war broke out against the Allies in 1941 and was drafted to Hong Kong as an Army interpreter for which he was so obviously fitted. As a near-civilian he was looked down upon by his fellow Japanese officers and was under continuous suspicion as he did not show hatred for the enemy and was thought to help individual prisoners and internees privately. This was true. When he heard of extreme cases of need he would use his own money and smuggle in special food and drugs which saved or alleviated many lives. We had a youth in his teens who came into camp with diabetes. The doctors had a stock of insulin to start with and were occasionally able to get more until none was left. It seemed certain that the lad would die. One of them was able to have a private word with Watanabe and he bought a supply on the black market in the city (he must have paid a wicked price). The lad survived to the end of camp but the sad part of the story is that he died on the ship on his way back to England because he had not allowed enough time to get adjusted to the richer food. Watanabe's act of compassion, however, for which he might well have been shot, is still remembered. So far as the church was concerned he was not allowed to fraternize with us but he did come to our Sunday School Party one Christmas and sang Japanese hymns that they would be singing in his own country. It was a moving experience for us as it was for him.

I like to remember him as a fellow Christian minister who broke local army regulations when he thought it right but was at all times loyal to his country and indeed was a credit to it. At the end of the war one of his two daughters wrote a letter to tell him of the death of her sister and of her mother. They were both blotted out by the first atom bomb. Watanabe was left with the metal fitting of his wife's handbag and a distorted piece of metal which had been part of her sewing machine, nothing more except happy memories of their earlier life as a family and his Christian faith. In a letter he once wrote, 'It was only when I was 17 that I found Jesus. I try hard to follow Jesus but I do not always succeed.' It is the opinion of hundreds of Britishers that he succeeded in a remarkable way.

Some years after the war a biography of John Watanabe, *Small Man of Nanataki* was written by Liam Nolan and published by Peter Davies.

10 · VJ Day

Japan surrendered on 14 August 1945, and the news was broadcast on the 15th, but we did not realize it at the time. It was clear that things were going badly for the Japanese when they began digging 'fox-holes' in the rocky surrounds of our camp. It was one of the features of the Pacific war that in the later stages they dug these 'fox-holes' in which men were ordered to hold out to the death. The prospect of our camp turning into a battleground alarmed us and we hoped that the allies would not choose our beach to land on! Odd things had begun to happen. On 10 August a hundred and fifty technicians with their wives and children were told to leave camp for an unknown destination. On 14 August a mysterious plane attacked and sank a small auxiliary vessel just off our camp and machine-gunned survivors in the water. On 15 August we began getting extra rations. On this day or the day after someone in the prison which some of our flats overlooked was recognized as a Turk who before the war had run a cafe in Hong Kong. He was pretending to write something on the outside wall of his cell which was interpreted by some as saying that Japan had surrendered. Whether there was in fact a radio still hidden in the camp or whether the Turk gave further information, there was talk of a special bomb and some of the more scientifically minded among us told us that the possibility of an atom bomb had been talked about before we entered camp.

On 17 August there was an air of suppressed excitement and rumours of peace gained strength. Later in the day Japanese newspapers came in to say that Japan had accepted the Potsdam Conference terms and surrendered on the 14th. An Imperial Rescript had been signed ordering the cessation of hostilities. Like a modern Moses, Mr Gimson, the Colonial Secretary, went

57

up the hill to confer with the Japanese Commandant and came down the hill with an official announcement that Japan had surrendered and that he had accepted responsibility for the good order of the camp. He appealed to all of us to back him up. The same day (17 August) at 6.30 p.m. we had our Thanksgiving Service in St Stephen's Hall. That day also tins of mutton were sent into camp by the Japanese (one tin per four persons), together with 'siege biscuits' and extra rice. That evening rice was going begging, not to mention spinach and uncooked potato tops. We dug up some sweet potatoes in the communal garden to add to the feast. That evening a squad of our police was sent out to guard the perimeter fence. It was clear that the Japanese authorities were trying to make up to us (a few days later they even produced some American toilet rolls – our 'victory rolls' as we called them with due respect for the RAF). Up the road beyond the prison however were the barracks of Japanese soldiers, now confined to their quarters. We wondered how they would take surrender and, of course, we could have done nothing against them. It says something for the Japanese army discipline that they remained quiet in their quarters for the fortnight or so before the British navy arrived.

The Pacific Ocean is a vast place. It was sixteen days after the surrender that the British fleet arrived and that was a day or two earlier than was originally thought possible. The interval was in part a tense period of waiting but at the same time a period of great activity, confusion bordering on anarchy at times, and a sense of elation and excitement – a curious mixture. To start with we were once again linked to the BBC news. Two radios were brought into camp at an early stage but often the newscaster seemed to be as confused as we were. Rumours abounded. We were not sure who would be coming – Americans, British or even the Nationalist Chinese army. It was suggested that a kite was being flown by the Chinese Government at Chungking that it would be fitting for the colony to be rehabilitated as a part of China, to which of course geographically it has always belonged. After a few days the BBC made it clear that it would be relieved by the British navy and re-established as a British Colony. So far as we could tell, the Japanese army officers behaved well and kept

58

a reasonable amount of order on the island but it was confusing for them. Representatives of the (pre-war) Hong Kong Government, many from our own camp, were turning up unannounced to see what the situation was and to see if any useful arrangements on their part could carry weight. Sundry others, again some from our camp, were wandering about on their own account. The position at the camp was clear that no one should attempt to leave the camp unless sent by Mr Gimson and the Camp Council on special assignments. But was this a strong recommendation or an order and on what authority? The delicate nature of the situation for a few days was perhaps expressed by the fact that when Mr Gimson, as Colonial Secretary, signed the notice about the cessation of hostilities on 17 August he signed it as 'Representative of Internees'. Fortunately the vast majority of the people had the sense to do what they were told. Bert Alton, with his excellent command of the Cantonese dialect, was sent out on a number of occasions, the first being with two others to arrange for fish to be sent into the camp as part of our rations. He was also able to re-establish contact with the Chinese Methodist Church. J. E. Sandbach was another of our missionaries who took part in these early tentative missions. For my part I was to stay in camp to make myself generally useful and was given the honour of being made a 'Blockhead' in charge of Block A1, an office which someone now upgraded to 'Block Representative'.

While very few were allowed to go out, very many were allowed in. There was almost an invasion from the Shamshuipo Prisoners-of-War Camp. They came on odd motorbikes, cars, lorries and a few by sea. One arrived on a fire engine with a Chinese fireman. Very soon two buses a day had been arranged to bring them. They arrived at 10.00 and 2.00, leaving at 12.00 and 4.00. They were nearly all husbands meeting their wives again for the first time since the war started. It was an emotional occasion. It was a moving sight of a very different kind to see wives around who had no husbands to come back to them. A terrible tragedy lay behind many of them. In October 1942 the Japanese had put a large number of the prisoners-of-war on the 'Lisbon Maru' to transfer them to Japan. It was sunk by a United States submarine with the loss of over eight hundred of our prisoners-of-war, many of whom had been battened down in the holds. To add to the tragedy, the wives were unable for many months to find out who had drowned and who had survived.

But the picture would not be complete without a further word on food. The Japanese yet again increased our daily ration of rice and beans. We had more tins of corned mutton. They gave us sweet potatoes and much else. On one day they sent in fifteen live pigs and, next day, one pound per head of meat. Friends sent in food even though they themselves must have been half-starving. Some went out to buy food for themselves and their families or friends. The extra food plus the news produced in us a dangerous kind of elation. Two things happened. We had energy before the body was ready for it. As early as 21 August a dance was held in St Stephen's Hall, something unthinkable a week earlier. We were told by our doctors of the need for adjusting to new and richer food gradually but we suddenly had new cases of beri-beri and stomach upsets of all sorts. Our teeth were not used to some of the new food and we ran temperatures for no apparent reason. I remember a junior doctor greeting the senior Professor of Surgery with, 'Good morning, Professor, how's the belly?' This was not only indicative of familiarity but also of a question that most people in camp were asking themselves and others. But we survived, and on 27 August I recorded in my diary: 'Bacon and egg for tiffin (lunch).' What more could a man want?

Still keeping to food, on 29 August we had the bizarre experience of being bombed from the air with food. The Indian Quarters were grouped around a large open space of what was once pleasant grass. Allied planes (presumably from an aircraft carrier) came over and, after circling round a number of times, parachuted crates of drugs and food to us. We had not been in such danger for a long time. Fortunately we got the idea in time and, more difficult, got the children under cover so that no one was hurt. A few of the crates hit roofs and buildings but most landed on the target area. That evening we sighted the British fleet on the horizon waiting to come into Hong Kong harbour in the morning.

The next morning, Thursday 30 August, the fleet sailed into Hong Kong harbour but of that we saw nothing as it was the other (northern) side of the island. In the afternoon three of us had a picnic on a beach just outside the perimeter of the camp. We got back to find that Admiral Sir Cecil Harcourt, Commander in Chief and the new Governor of Hong Kong, was expected. He arrived about 5.00 p.m. in the centre of three 'jeeps', the first and the third being the only bodyguard he had. We were both surprised and impressed that he had had the courage to come through the island with so little protection. We had a short ceremony in which the Union Jack was raised and Captain Shadwell of the Maidstone brought us up to date with the news. The next day HMS Freemantle, an Australian mine-sweeper, anchored in the bay for a couple of hours and gave a lavish welcome to internees who were able to swim out or were taken on board in the ship's launch. The hospital ship 'Oxfordshire' was by now in Hong Kong harbour and took on board some sixty of our most serious hospital cases.

As I have said, I was confined to barracks and saw at first hand only what happened in the camp. I had come off the sweet potato gardeners' squad some time before and was now on a kitchen staff. On Monday 3 September, I suddenly saw the lanky figure of Dr Moore (known affectionately by his Chinese name of 'Mooi'), one of our missionary doctors, casually walking along outside our block. The arrival of the Man in the Moon would scarcely have surprised me more. He had been in Free China at our Shiukwaan (Kukong) Hospital and later had joined the British Army Aid Group, a mysterious body which seems to have had the run of Free China for many kinds of helpful purposes. He had arrived the day before by air from Kumming and had been sent to assist prisoners-of-war and internees. Among other things he later took over responsibility for the hospital and arranged a relief staff of six army Sisters and VADs from Leyte in the Philippines (don't ask me how they came into the picture!) and who provided much-needed help for our own matron and sisters who had coped so nobly for three and a half years.

I did, however, have one private escapade. Two days later I was going round making a list of women and children who wished to be repatriated (many of course were Hong Kong Chinese and Eurasians) and I fell on some concrete steps and damaged my

61

knee. Now let me phrase the rest of the story rather carefully! There was in the harbour a New Zealand hospital ship, the 'Maunganui'. A New Zealand doctor in camp examined my knee and felt that an X-ray would be advisable. He also felt it would be advisable for my New Zealand friend, Jack Johnston, of Queen Mary Hospital days, and co-worker in the camp, to go with me. There was now an 8.30 a.m. bus to town which we took next morning. An ambulance took us to the Naval Dockyard and a launch from HMS Maidstone took us to the hospital ship. It was priority treatment all along the line. After the X-ray we were able to visit Stanley Internment Camp patients who were already on board and the Padre invited us to have lunch with him and the officers. After three and a half years in internment I was astounded at the vitality of all we met and also at the speed with which they got through the meal. They were possibly surprised at the poor appetites we seemed to have as internees. The truth is we were handicapped by such talking as we had to engage in and more particularly by our inability to take in that kind of food other than slowly. When we were the only two remaining at table apart from our host we felt that in all decency we had to give up and leave. To this day, when I feel that there is something missing in my life, I think of a most intriguing sweet consisting of ice-cream-plus which I had to leave as a mere name on the menu. Perhaps I should confess that the X-ray showed no fracture, it was simply a bad sprain.

To close down this part of my story let me briefly explain that the most seriously ill patients from both camps were put on board the 'Maunganui' which was going to Taiwan (then Formosa) to pick up more. The 'Empress of Australia', then a troopship, anchored off-shore after landing the troops she had brought and took on board the women and children, together with such men as wanted to go and were willing to accept troop deck accommodation. We left on 11 September. The life of the colony had to be got going again and that meant that some men and women with responsibility for administration, Government departments, business and commerce had to stay behind. They were scarcely fit for responsibility but they did a surprisingly good job as many of us discovered when we got back. The same applied to the English

Methodist Church and the Sailors' and Soldiers' Home. In my case it was decided that J. E. Sandbach, who was in charge of our English and Chaplaincy work, should stay on for a few months and that I should return to England with a view to taking his place temporarily after what would be a normal furlough of twelve months.

11 · Westward Ho!

It was great to be going somewhere. Not even the Captain knew precisely where we were going. It was a time of juggling from day to day with all the available shipping in a vast area according to information continually coming in from internment camps throughout South-East Asia while bearing in mind women and children and others who had been evacuated to Australia and New Zealand!

The captain must have been a very patient man. Certainly he had much to contend with. His somewhat skeleton crew had only been able to do a rough clean-up after the troops left and before we were all sent on board. The troops were disciplined to obey orders and so was his crew but we were a pretty bolshy lot and looked it. We made ourselves at home as best we could. I was billeted on E deck near the ship's propellers. There were no fresh breezes there to mitigate the tropical heat and like most of the men I slept on deck at night and spent most of the day there as well. I remember the incident of the rolls. Travellers by boat will know that rolls are served with all main meals and the remains, sometimes whole rolls, are thrown through the porthole. Quite a furore arose among many of the internees when they saw bread, of which they had been starved for so many years, thrown to the fish. A delegation asked to see the captain, who wisely agreed to meet them, heard their case and gave orders to the stewards to dispose of no more food in this way. It was a sign of something. I suppose that mentally we were not adjusted to normal living.

On 13 September we found ourselves in Manila Bay, an

enormous area of water so extensive that we could not see land. Whether there was some mist as well I cannot remember. It was studded with scores of ships, mainly passenger/troopships and large ones at that. Later in the afternoon we proceeded to a wharf and were welcomed by a band. The Canadians on board and the POWs, except for husbands with wives on board, disembarked and were taken to a camp in Red Cross ambulances. On the 15th we pulled away to our old position in the bay and awaited orders. Later that afternoon we moved back into the inner harbour and tied up to an old wreck. A squad of Filipinos was sent on board to clean up the troop decks. We also had various issues from the Red Cross – towels for women and children, combs, flannels and slippers for men, dresses and shirts for girls and boys, plus tins of grapefruit juice all round. Meantime the Maunganui turned up again and Jack Johnston managed to get on board. He came back with grim stories told by the patients who had been prisoners-of-war in Taiwan (Formosa). It was obvious that conditions there had been as bad as any in the Far East.

The departure of our POWs meant that our numbers were reduced from something like 1,790 to 1,000 of which some 600 were women and children, all of us from Stanley. Sunday was like old times! – 6.45 a.m., Communion Service; 10.00 a.m., Morning Worship taken by Bert Alton and the sermon by Ken Dow. On 18 September we took on board some 1,200 troops who had been POWs in Japan or Taiwan. They had been flown in from Okinawa and had been at a rest camp near Manila. In theory the POWs were segregated from the civilians, the POWs having the port side of the promenade deck and the civilians the starboard side. All right in theory but each evening it was remarkable how crowded the starboard side was and how few were on the port side! Next day we transferred fifteen more cases to the Maunganui and on 20 September sailed for Singapore.

At Singapore a hundred or so bound for Australia and New Zealand left us, most to rejoin wives and families who had been evacuated from Hong Kong before the Far Eastern war. Some had already been flown to Australia from Manila. Before we left Singapore we had a flying visit from Lady Mountbatten. She was Superintendent-in-Chief of the St John's Ambulance Brigade and equally interested in the Red Cross and had been given by Lord Mountbatten a letter authorizing her to go anywhere to locate prisoner-of-war and internment camps and to visit them as she was able. She met the troops first and then the civilians. She told us what wonderful people we were, an idea that had not occurred to us before and which needed more than a few grains of salt, and then went on to tell us interesting bits about 'Louis' and the Burma campaign and the work of the Red Cross in the Far East. She was as thin as we were (or had been) and obviously wearing herself out in her varied activities. She had been in Java the day before. She had last been in England three weeks before and told us about the situation there. It was a refreshing shock to hear her exclaim, 'The Labour Party's in, thank God.' We were all very moved to think that she had taken time to visit an incredibly scruffy lot of civilians such as ourselves and it was an interesting example of how a notable individual of calibre can boost morale in a brief visit and an off-the-cuff address.

To hurry on, we were entertained in a camp outside Colombo by as smart a bunch of WRNS as you would hope to see, taken to a new camp at Suez to be equipped with winter clothes and welcomed by the Lord Mayor and a band as we came alongside at Liverpool. Poor battered Liverpool, but the welcome was cordial and the folk determined to make the best of the peace now offered. The city's motto was and is, 'Deus nobis haec otia fecit'. It was an emotional moment when I was welcomed at Euston station by my mother, sisters and brother. It seemed a little eerie that I was unable to recognize my own brother who was then aged twenty.

12 · Second Wind

Most of us were able to readjust remarkably speedily. After a month or so of relaxed living at home I was able to revert to the normal routine of a missionary on furlough. Visits to the Mission House in Marylebone Road aside, this meant taking 'Overseas

Missions Anniversaries' (as they were then called) at Methodist churches, usually on a Sunday or a weekend. I found myself at Richmond (London), Gantshill (London), Southport, St Annes, Spondon (Derby), Coulsdon (London), Norbury (London), Leeds, Stoke Newington and Mildmay Park (London) and Greenford. There was a Methodist Guild Guest Houses Reunion in Birmingham and Conferences for the Young Laymen's League (a young men's missionary movement), the Fellowship of the Kingdom (mainly Methodist ministers) and an Easter Missionary School. There was also a refreshing visit for a few days to Wesley House, my old theological college at Cambridge.

The highlights of the furlough for most of us China Missionaries was a 'Welcome Back' Public Meeting in the Westminster Central Hall. If I remember rightly there were over a hundred of us on the platform. It was certainly good to see each other but equally good to feel the interest and support of the audience, very many of whom had been remembering and praying for us during our internment in the camps. The highlight for me was the singing of Charles Wesley's hymn, 'Head of thy church triumphant'. He brought the Exodus crossing of the Red Sea and the fiery furnace of Daniel up to date in verses 2 and 3:

> The name we still acknowledge
> That burst our bonds asunder
> And loudly sing
> Our conquering King,
> In songs of joy and wonder.
> In every day's deliverance
> Our Jesus we discover
> 'Tis He, 'tis He
> That smote the sea
> and led us safely over!
>
> While in affliction's furnace
> And passing through the fire,
> Thy love we praise,
> Which knows our days
> And ever brings us nigher.
> We clap our hands exulting

In thine almighty favour;
The love divine
Which made us thine
Shall keep us thine for ever.

So the time came quickly for my return to Hong Kong. I was booked in the SS Otranto along with a complement of passengers some of whom were coming out for the first time but most represented Government, business and church personnel returning after leave and furlough to face the double challenge of restoring the old and developing the new in the light of a post-war world. We left on 14 September 1946.

On my arrival back in Hong Kong I was met again by Frank Evison (as I had been in 1938) who had come in from South China to help recover our property. During the war the Sailors' and Soldiers' Home had been taken over by the Japanese army and then after the war by the British Forces. Frank Evison had managed to get back the top (third) floor and was using it as a Missionary Guest House, thereby meeting an urgent need for all the Missionary Societies as accommodation was scarce and all were returning to their stations in China through Hong Kong. A small group of English Methodist laymen had already repaired the English Methodist Church and got Sunday services going. For the rest it was up to me with their invaluable co-operation. About this time James Lee turned up, a Chinese who had been in charge of the restaurant on the ground floor before the war. He was taken on again on the same terms which meant that it was his business but he had to hand over a percentage of his profits to the Home. One of my jobs was to receive each day all the bills of the previous day's takings and to spot-check them. The arrangement worked well. I remember the saga of the ice-cream. I should explain that our Methodist Sailors' and Soldiers' Home is built at the edge of the red light district of Wanchai and not far from us was the much larger and more pretentious building of the Fleet Club. We got on well together because we were so different. We were a church foundation and had a small chapel; moreover we had a rule that no alcoholic drink was to be served or consumed on the premises and the minister in charge lived in a flat built into the premises. There were always those in the Forces who preferred quieter premises for one reason or another and yet there was the healthy whiff of a certain rivalry between us. In the early days James Lee got hold of some tins of Australian ice-cream powder and produced an ice-cream that became known as the best in town so that we also had servicemen coming to us for this reason alone. Disaster came when he ran out of this particular ice-cream powder. For some weeks James Lee experimented with all sorts of ingredients and treatment. At one time he was putting pounds of butter in. In the end he produced an ice-cream that was up to scratch and we could all breathe again.

It was, of course, fascinating to meet and welcome missionaries of so many different denominations and countries. Some had brought their families; some were returning to old work in churches, hospitals, schools and universities and wisely were ascertaining conditions before allowing wives and children to rejoin them, and there were many single men and women. In the four months or so I was in charge, over a hundred and eighty people (including children) passed through and the list I have makes interesting reading still. Those going the furthest were, I think, Church of Scotland missionaries going back to Moukden. They had been interned in Japan in a building a mile or two from where one of the atomic bombs was dropped. The glass of every window in the building had been shattered but fortunately all had a wall between them and the devastation and had simply to survive the shock. Many, of course, were returning to nearby Kwangtung Province. They were all looking forward to meeting Chinese friends and colleagues again after such a long separation.

To re-open the rest of the building took longer but we were determined to re-open the first and second floors (the bedrooms, dormitories, quiet room-cum-chapel) in time for Christmas Day which would be the fifth anniversary of the surrender of Hong Kong to the Japanese. We managed it but it was hard work. A tribute to the British firm who made the steel windows (name to be revealed on receipt of an SAE!). In spite of years of neglect they were in excellent shape and only needed paint. Tribute to many individuals, of course, but the major tribute to the Royal Navy who backed us up to the hilt. They provided the beds.

68

Because we were serving the Forces they kept us stocked with unlimited supplies of chocolate etc. for a small shop that we ran in the entrance hall. In ways large and small they could not have been more helpful. Perhaps I ought to explain the post-war atmosphere in which we were working. There was still the vast relief of the end of both wars (West and East). There was enthusiasm engendered in all who were engaged in rebuilding what had been destroyed whether they were re-establishing private business and enterprises or setting up once more the various Government Departments (Administration, Public Works, the Medical Services, Postal and Telephone Services etc.). It was satisfying in the extreme to see Hong Kong come to life again and men and women worked incredibly long hours in what in other circumstances might be dubbed as unfair exploitation. In my own small corner I myself reckoned that I have never worked so hard and that I survived because I had the restaurant below me and, by no means least, the chocolate I could so freely buy in my comings and goings! There was no nonsense. After all they had been through, nobody was willing to put up with any red tape. Government servants took upon themselves full authority and worked on the basis of common sense. Others in commerce and industry did the same. They served the interests of others often far away and, ignoring the minutiae of consultation with boards and committees, they did the job so well that complaints when they came were minimal. An illustration in minor key was similar action in which I was involved with the backing of an excellent committee of laymen behind me. We discovered that our account in the Hong Kong and Shanghai Bank was intact with a substantial sum in credit. We spent it all on repainting and re-equipping our Sailors' and Soldiers' Home and appealed to our London Headquarters for more. Eyebrows were raised but they sent £4,000 which was quite a sum in those days. It was invigorating to be trusted and to report what we had done rather than what we proposed to do. To give another example, we had to check with the Government the registration of all churches and chapels. I discovered that our English Methodist Church was still registered in the previous century's name of 'The Wesleyan Methodist Church and Garrison Chapel'. Over the phone it was changed to what everybody thought it was and I do not know to this day whether the change has ever been noted and approved by our London Headquarters! We all had a job to do and we got on with it.

In all this it was, of course, helpful to have got to know in the Internment Camp so many people with authority in civil life in Hong Kong. I remember a New Zealand doctor and his wife who stayed in our Missionary Guest House. Within a few hours of arrival he developed appendicitis and by phoning a fellow internee who was now back in the Queen Mary Hospital I was able to get him into hospital in double-quick time. It was also interesting to know some of the European police so well. I remember in particular one memorable contact. I have already explained that we were (deliberately) built at the beginning of the red light district. In the earlier days after the war the problem of prostitution was particularly pressing and I was always phoning up the police to ask them to clear the pavements. After trying the patience of the police for some weeks I had a phone call from them: 'We are very busy people and we can't spend our time chasing your prostitutes.' The message was clear but it left me with a dilemma. In the end I went over to the prostitutes and explained my difficulties while they indicated theirs. We reached that day what I suppose could be called a sort of 'gentleman's agreement' that if they came over to our side of the road I would call the police but if they stayed on the other side I would not. It was a most happy compromise which served my time and, I hope, my successor's as well.

Those were halcyon days which could not last and which nobody wanted to last. I suppose this might help to explain why, as a pacifist from student days, I was looking after a Sailors' and Soldiers' Home. In 1946 we never envisaged the one hundred and fifty or so wars that have occurred since (both civil and international). To one degree or another the whole world was weary of war and exhausted. The navy, the army and the RAF were necessary as a police force but no longer as a war machine. I suppose that was part of my thinking. Another factor was that of course all missionaries were 'pacifists' in the sense that we never resorted to force. There was, I think, a third factor. In these days

I suppose the earlier connotation of 'pacifist' had fallen into disuse and dissenters now dissociate themselves from the far more dangerous preparation for nuclear warfare. I do not remember in my Hong Kong days the kind of unhealthy and emotional reaction to such dissenters by politicians, armchair critics and a section of the people as a whole that was found in England then and is found in England now. I suppose I was never a very virulent pacifist. When normal transport was non-existent I travelled between Hong Kong and Canton on a gunboat by courtesy of the Navy. I respected their position while those who gave the matter any thought respected mine. Likewise when the 'Belfast' was in harbour I was entirely happy about going on board to give the cadets (if I have the name right) a lesson in Chinese!

On one occasion I went up to Canton accompanied by Albert Ball, a British army padre. He was a fellow Methodist minister who hoped to get a break from Hong Kong and see something of our church work as well as the sights and the people of a Chinese city. His commanding officer granted him leave of absence on condition that he went in full uniform 'to show the flag'. Those were still days after the war when neither Chinese nor 'foreigners' could lay claim to smart clothes. In a crowded Canton bus he stood out like someone from Mars in his resplendent and well-tailored uniform. I happened to hear one Chinese say to a friend, 'Who the heck is he?' (or words to that effect). After a pause his friend answered, 'He must belong to the Salvation Army'. I hope the padre had the courage to tell his commanding officer when he got back.

On an equally light note but with sombre overtones, I am reminded of an incident later on when I had moved up to Kukong. The countryside was much disturbed by robbers and the local police decided that they could no longer guarantee our safety (we were on the opposite bank of the river to the town). They gave us six rifles and some bullets and wished us well. One night there was a disturbance in the lane between us and the Boys' School and I walked over to our wall to see what was happening. Fortunately the moon gave me enough light to spot our hospital lab-technician pointing one of those rifles at me. I suppose I could

71

claim this as the most dangerous moment of my not-uneventful life!

Meantime life at the Sailors' and Soldiers' Home was settling down to a steady routine. A Wing who had been 'No. 1 Boy' before the war, had turned up. I remembered him as a big sturdy figure. I think his family originally came from North China. I was appalled to see him so emaciated and spiritless. He had had a hard time. We were glad to give him a rehabilitation grant and take him on again and he was soon back to his old self. Our staffing was now adequate.

Jim Curry, an RN chaplain, was stationed in Hong Kong and we found room for him in 'the flat' which was in fact a two-storey section of the Home so that when his wife and two children, Judith and Tim (now a well-known actor), arrived later there was room for all. J. E. Sandbach returned in May 1947 to take over the Home and the English Methodist Church. That took the load off my shoulders and I now looked forward to a job in China proper for the first time since my arrival in 1938.

It was not to be. Donald Childe now Missionary Society Representative, asked me to stay on for a couple of months to put right our two looted and vandalized properties, the holiday bungalow at Cheung Chau and the little mountain shack up Laan Tau. This was a tricky but delightful job, very different from the strain of getting the Home going. So far as the Cheung Chau bungalow was concerned I think that there had been a tub outside to collect rainwater but it seemed to me that while we were at it (and the bungalow really was in a mess) it would be a good idea to have some running water to the kitchen and the toilet. I approached one of our Methodist members who was in the Public Works Department and he approved the idea. He drew a plan and wrote down all necessary details for the making of a watertight concrete tank including some additive which I quite forget. I memorized what I could and took notes with me when I went to interview the only Chinese builder of any repute on the island. I spoke with such authority as I could muster. He probably realized that I was a complete ignoramus, but we agreed a price and the job was eventually done. To my vast relief the tank held water and the plumbing was adequate. I still shudder to think of the

72

comments that would have been made in many quarters had the heart of the bungalow been a leaky tank.

The Laan Tau shack was simpler because it was smaller. At least one other shack had been repaired with windows of small panes of very thick glass to save the need for the heavy wooden typhoon shutters. We followed suit and, so far as I can remember, we also installed a more modest running-water system supplied from roof rain. Visits in May and June to the sea breezes of Cheung Chau and the cooler air of Laan Tau were delightful but at last I was released and prepared to leave for Kukong where I was stationed.

13 · Crooked River

I was looking forward to Kukong, today called once again Shiakwan (Shaoguan). It was further into rural China to start with. In my mind it had a young vigorous image. The hospital was a daughter of the senior hospital at Fatshan. Our Ying Kwong boys' school was next door and here our Wa Ying school had refugeed. There were fascinating stories I had heard of earlier days both of Kukong itself and of the North River Methodist Circuit in general which stretched some forty miles north to Lok Cheung and sixty miles south to Ying Tak. Except for a short time just before the end of the war it had remained in Free China and since I shall have no other opportunity to pay tribute to the Chinese Postal Service let me do it here. An Imperial Courier Service for carrying official documents may well date from the second millennium BC. It probably began to carry private mail in the Ming Dynasty (1368–1644). The official Imperial Post Office was established under a foreign Inspector-general of Customs in 1896. It had a most honourable pedigree which I had occasion to test when I was in Japanese occupied Canton before Pearl Harbour and wanted to post two books I had borrowed to their owner in Kukong in Free China. It seemed a bit like asking the Post Office in London if I could post two books to Warsaw during the war. However, I consulted an official in Canton Post Office and after careful thought he said, 'Leave it to me, sir,' whereupon I bought the stamps and posted the parcel. When the war was over I met the owner of the books and he assured me that the books had got through and in quite a short space of time. Well done, the Post Office.

So on 19 July I sailed for Canton on the river steamer 'Wusueh' with some twenty-two pieces of luggage, a shocking amount for an ex-internee who survived for nearly four years on a suitcase and a couple of blankets. After a pleasant weekend in Canton I found myself and my baggage on board a small towboat bound up the North River for Kukong. As good fortune would have it, there was a Sister returning to Kukong Hospital and she looked after my welfare. It took three days and three nights to do the one hundred and forty miles to our destination as in summer the river is in flood and I was on the towboat itself, so called because these river boats nearly always towed another boat with freight behind. There was a Leyland engine amidships and over this the main passenger accommodation, which consisted of two long wooden shelves where each staked his claim to one of the rush mats provided. In front was the cabin for the man in charge (there seemed to be no captain in our sense). Round the whole boat was a gangway three planks wide where it was delightful to stand in the early morning or evening. I was provided with a hot bath each evening (in the two and a half-foot square lavatory) and when we arrived at Kukong they were kind enough to drop off the nurse and myself and our luggage at the hospital even though it took careful manoeuvring. At that point the boat at full throttle barely held its own against the current. Darkness added to our difficulties but all went well. It had been a delightful trip proceeding slowly but surely past villages and farms and with time to stare and meditate and perchance to dream.

The hospital compound was surrounded by a wall and a ring of poinsettias which someone years before had planted. It must have been a major task but the poinsettia grows out of doors in South China and it provided a mass of red flowers (leaves, I am told) each Christmas, red being the happy colour in China – 'the Christmas flower' is what they called it. I was given a bungalow in the south of the compound and near the school and had no sooner settled in than I was off again. I was due for a holiday and had no intention of missing my first chance of seeing something of China outside Hong Kong and Canton. Kuling on the Yangtse sounded a place to visit. It was a mountain resort started by missionaries for health reasons some fifty years before, not unlike Laan Tau in this respect but vastly superior and more spacious.

This meant going by train to Hankow. Remember that this was still only two years after the end of the war. With Chinese ingenuity steel bridges that had been blown up in the war were being replaced by temporary all-wood bridges made of intricate scaffolding of tree trunks. They had to take the enormously heavy USA railway engines that UNRRA (United Nations Relief and Rehabilitation Administration) was sending over. It was incredible to me how these bridges took the strain but they always did – well, not quite always! Under the circumstances trains could not always run to time and I started at Kukong by catching the express train of the day before. I must have travelled first class for I remember comfortable seats, endless drinks of tea and hand towels wrung out in warm water that attendants offered throughout the day to refresh face and hands. I remember also a kind act of Chinese courtesy. We had to stop for several hours at one small town and a business man in my compartment, seeing that I was on my own, insisted on taking me to a restaurant he knew and standing me an excellent and most welcome meal. I hoped the train would not leave without us and it didn't. We had to change trains once somewhere by the Tung Ting lake, an amazing inland sea though the traveller cannot appreciate its size as you are unable to see the other side. I remember that they went to no end of trouble to get all the first class carriages at the back, the reason being that robbers were always supposed to attack the engine first and then work their way down the train. Robbers of many kinds and dispositions were a fact of life until the Communists arrived. I never heard of any robbers attacking a train from the rear. I suppose they could not run fast enough and perhaps they felt it to be cheating to buy tickets lower down the line and board the train as passengers, although this had long been commonplace on ships at sea.

In forty-eight hours we reached Wuchang which together with Hanyang and Hankow makes up the city of Wuhan which most of us call Hankow. I was met by Jack Chamberlayne whom I remembered as a champion swimmer at the City of London School and I was put up at the Union Theological College which was still something of a mess although a lot of repair work had already been done. After a day or so's respite I was booked on a river boat going down the Yangtse which left at 2.00 a.m. Aided by the current the boat reached Kiukiang (Jiujiang) by late afternoon. I found a coolie willing to take me up the mountain at once and reached the camp and my host and hostess, Bernard and Marjorie Redhead, soon after dark. I later discovered that so far as people could remember I was the first person to do the whole trip in one day. I wonder whether the record still stands!

As I have indicated, Kuling was much more developed than Laan Tau and vast by comparison. A Chinese village had grown up in a dip at the top and bungalows and houses were spread out at the head of the several valleys. It was a lovely and refreshing spot, delightfully cool after the summer heat below. Chiang Kai-Shek had a bungalow just below where I was staying and I believe we were renting two other bungalows to Madame, though neither was in residence. I was interested to discover the very informal and friendly terms on which the older missionaries were with the Chiang Kai-Sheks who each year made a point of themselves visiting quite a number. Those two hard-pressed people benefited from the change as much as any of us. The Sunday morning service at the 'Union Church' was not only a time of worship and real inspiration but it was also moving to look round and see men and women of so many denominations, so many age groups, so many parts of China and to reflect on the varied experiences represented in that small building.

It was for me a memorable holiday. We had good food, good company and good exercise, walks and climbs, swimming, tennis, tea-parties, dinner parties and concerts. But of course it soon passed. After three weeks Dr George Pearson and Paul Jefferies, both of our Hunan District, decided to try a new way home and I elected to join them. We went by train from Kiukiang to Nanchang, the capital of Kiangsi (Jiangxi), where we stayed two nights with the American Methodists. Then it was country bus to Changsha, the capital of Hunan. I had by then developed a boil (rich living on the mountain?) which in itself was bad enough but what made it worse was that it was on my bottom. I had Dr Pearson to attend to it at the end of the day and to cut a painful story short we reached Changsha safely, where I stayed with John Foster a few days to recuperate and then by train back to Kukong. It was at Changsha that quite by chance I bumped into the Rev. and Mrs Etling and was able to thank them for the food parcels sent to us in Stanley Internment Camp.

Let me say more about Kukong. It means 'crooked river' and is built between two rivers at a point where they join on their way south to Canton. Here was our main church with ancillary premises including a shop front where evangelistic services were held looking on the street. The superintendent of the circuit, the Rev. Huen Fung-Sheung, a Chinese, lived on the premises and made me welcome from the start. On the west bank of the main river lay more houses and a number of farms and these were normally connected to the town by a bridge consisting of sampans tied up side by side. The hospital and the school were on the west bank a little further down. The whole valley was intensively farmed but if you climb a hilltop behind the hospital you can view mountains as far as you can see – and I was told that they go all the way to the east coast of China. Probably every valley is cultivated and that is where the villages were – and the village chapels – living their own lives but appallingly at the mercy of any unruly armed gang.

14 · Back on the Job

When I returned the hospital was running under an entirely Chinese staff but Dr John Rose divided his time between Kukong and Fatshan. Before long Dr Peter Early (coming to us from a Friends' Ambulance Unit in West China) and Dr Clifford Austin joined the Chinese doctors. The Chinese matron (now, we hear, a doctor) had been well-trained at Fatshan and was doing an excellent job. I was chaplain to the hospital and school and took a minor part in the town church, e.g. by taking services and preaching (which took a lot of time by way of preparation). In this I was schooled by my language teacher who was a Chinese minister recovering from TB. Very recently I was delighted to hear that he is still alive and in charge of the first church to be reopened in Fatshan – 'post-denominational' of course these days. I also took simple English classes for the nurses which were conversational and very down to earth. They had to know, for example, in English as well as in Chinese anything from the names of the various worms that can flourish in our intestines to technical terms for many kinds of operations. I acquired quite a bit of medical knowledge myself as a by-product. It was also interesting to realize that many or most of our English medical terms are two Greek words (occasionally Latin) put together into one word that most of us use without understanding the original. Chinese translates the original two words with the result that the original meaning is not lost. They also caught me out on one or two curious Victorianisms that I had never realized were curious at all. They were, for example, vastly amused when we discussed the important matter of finding the toilets in an English hospital or town. I had to explain that (in those days) they might not find what they wanted under 'MEN' or 'WOMEN' but under 'GENTLEMEN' or 'LADIES', and had to explain why and what the difference was anyhow. I also had to act as an apologist for the way in which we English were far too shy to use any word for the main object of a so-called toilet but suggested what we meant by reverting to the idea of washing (lavatory, latrine, water closet) or the idea of tidying one's hair (toilet). The Chinese of course name (in two crisp words) the place in question in a perfectly respectable and matter-of-fact way. We also occasionally had fun when they (with the Chinese word in front of them) had to demonstrate to me what exactly an English word meant. They took their studies seriously, though, as may be shown by the fact that in the year that I arrived at Kukong six nurses from our Training School took the first five and seventh places in the Final Examination for the province of Kwangtung. All the time, of course, I had to wrestle with biblical Chinese, newspaper Chinese and conversational Chinese and take prayers as well as give sermons.

As my bungalow was inside the hospital compound I was able to take a fairly full part in hospital activities and was allowed to watch a number of operations. The most remarkable operation was on a desperately ill patient from the mountains who came in with a huge ovarian cyst. The operation was successful. After a few weeks she was weighed and the cyst was found to have been slightly heavier than the patient! She came into hospital as an apparently old woman and she left months later looking her true age of seventeen. For a detailed account written by the surgeon concerned see *Appendix A*.

More about the hospital later. Let me now return to the railway on which I had to travel so often. It was the Canton–Hankow Railway so called because, a trifle illogically, it ended at Wuchang. I have mentioned the astonishing way in which Chinese coolies with their hands and the simplest of tools were getting it going again, spanning rivers with scaffolding of tree trunks that could take the largest, oldest and clumsiest locomotive from the USA. The trains themselves gradually sorted themselves out in new railway jargon. There was the 'special express' such as the Hankow express which I usually got from Canton. This normally left at 10.00 p.m. and (bridges and robbers permitting) got to Kukong about 6.30 a.m. the next day. I tended to take visitors on this train who included, I well remember, a certain Miss Horrex. Chinese, as you know, have great difficulty in pronouncing 'r' and substitute 'l' in its place. Everyone she met would call her Miss Ho(r)licks. She was on the consular staff in Canton and had to get the permission of the Consul General. It turned out afterwards that he had misheard Kukong as Hong Kong and was under the impression that she was in the latter place. Then there was the 'ordinary express' which was recommended for more local travel. The 'lightweight express' was interesting because it was left behind by the Japanese. It was in fact a converted lorry with either two or three lightweight, toy-like carriages behind. On one occasion when Dr John Rose was travelling in it, it was challenged by a water buffalo. Unfortunately the driver sounded his horn and the water buffalo accepted the challenge and charged. The 'lorry' was derailed and the buffalo was killed. Coolies appeared out of the apparently empty countryside and lifted the lorry back on the rails. I always feel particularly sad about this story because I am sure that if someone could have explained to the buffalo that the driver meant no harm, the accident would not have occurred. The last category of trains was the 'goods and passengers mixed' train. This was not an express, far from it.

Those were very uncertain days in the countryside. The Communist armies were pushing inexorably down from the north. Units of the Nationalist forces were liable to be around as were armed bands who claimed to represent the Communists (and rarely did). Then there were the bands whom I have called 'robbers' some of whom may have had political ideas of one sort or another but most were out to rob and pillage. The villages had to put up with whoever came their way. This is why I never managed to reach all the churches in our circuit! I did, however, get around to most when things were quieter.

Lok Cheung, some forty miles up the railway from Kukong, was a place that I was able to visit several times. The first time was in September 1947 when I went up with Mr Huen (the Superintendent Minister of the Circuit) for the opening of the new church. A faithful catechist was in charge whom most of us knew as 'The Buffalo'. He was thickset and slow-moving, not up to the requirements of a candidate for the ministry but capable of looking after a small town congregation. The next time I went up I thought it would be good to have some evening evangelistic meetings and he agreed. I had acquired a film-strip projector and a mixture of film-strips, some biblical, some about the church and the church's message and some from the British Consulate. There was no electricity. Later I acquired a car accumulator and later still a car headlight and six dry batteries but on this occasion I did a Heath Robinson job with a KLIM (powdered milk) tin and a pressurized paraffin lamp. The shiny round interior of the milk tin did something to gather and reflect the light. The result in that church was a pretty poor picture but it sufficed with a running commentary by the catechist. The church was full each night.

The audience lapped up anything that we could show them. The Buffalo somehow managed to bring all together into a coherent Christian message (in ways that would have surprised the British Council). I still vividly remember the end of the final meeting when I was showing the story of the Prodigal Son. The catechist, poor man, had a bad attack of gout and had been walking with the aid of a stick. He accompanied the film-strip with a moving explanation of the parable, getting more and more enthusiastic every moment. He ended by waving his stick in the air along with his hands and using it to point to the figures on the screen so that no one could possibly be fooled by the poor presentation. His gout was temporarily quite forgotten. I left him next morning to gather the fruits of the meetings and went my way in the knowledge that buffaloes can move at great speed when the spirit moves them.

My last trip to Lok Cheung was in the early months of 1949 when the Communist armies were pushing south rapidly. I got there all right by train but there was no possibility of returning the same way. Every train was crowded to capacity with refugees on the roofs of carriages and even standing on the buffers between the carriages. Fortunately I was able to find a boatman who was willing to take me back to Kukong by the river. It was the time when Chiang Kai-Shek was throwing his last dice. The paper currency having reached the end of the road (who wants a ten-million dollar note if nobody will accept it?), he minted real silver dollars. I paid three of these dollars which the boatman was glad to have because it was real money whatever the future might hold. The river was much narrower up there but even so I was not expecting the rapids which he negotiated with great skill. I got back to Kukong safely and it was good to be home.

Another memorable trip was to Ying Tak in September 1948. This was a sizeable town some sixty miles south on the way to Canton and a natural centre for a wide area around. Here I met three German ladies from the Lutheran church and their Chinese minister, Father Tong of the local Roman Catholic church, a Mr Wong who was in charge of the Baptist church and two members of the Church of Christ in China. I was staying with our own catechist who had promised to take me to as many of the small village churches as possible. He did his best to reassure me about the trip by explaining that one of the two main bands of 'robbers' in the area was led by two Methodist Local (lay) Preachers whom he knew personally. I appreciated his thoughtfulness and forbore from enquiring whether they were still in membership! Next morning we were up early and took a small boat up the Yung Kong river which flowed fairly swiftly between steep cliffs. It was a delightful day, I remember. We reached Wong Kong, a picturesque walled and palisaded village with three gates which were guarded at night by a 'Self-Preservation Corps'. Actually the wall consisted mainly of the walls of buildings at the edge of the village. Our Methodist Chapel was at a corner of the wall and so was in a key position. Unfortunately the toilet was outside the wall which made it awkward after dark. You had to approach the sentry on the nearby door and say, 'Please may I go to the toilet?' To which he would reply, 'Pass, friend, but don't be long' – or words to that effect! We found our chapel occupied by the guards but we were able to hold a Communion Service next morning. After rice we left on foot for Tsak Tong which we reached after two hours' walk on a hot summer's day. We had tea and a gruel of rice, peanuts and taro and pushed on to Sheung Taai which we reached just as it was getting dark. There was only time for rice, family prayers and bed.

Next morning we had a Communion Service and then rice. We had planned to go on to In Leng but were told it was not safe as Government troops had just withdrawn from the area. So it was a four and a half-hour walk back to Tsak Tong where we spent the night. There was a rumour of strange men having been seen in the valley and the village suddenly froze when some claimed to see people walking in the dark on the hill opposite (the custom was that *bona fide* travellers, if they had to travel in the dark, always carried a light), but nothing untoward happened. Next day was Sunday and we got back to Ying Tak by 11.50 to find that a Communion Service was arranged and took place at 12.30, which I thought was a quick piece of work. On the Monday we took a boat to Hoh Tau and walked to Mong Fau where we discovered the premises were occupied by soldiers and could do little about it. So we headed back to Hoh Tau on the railway where I had left my two cases, and home to Kukong. It had been good to share the Lord's Supper with so many faithful members and to understand better the difficulties and dangers they were having to face.

15 · A Holiday that was Different

Before I lose sight of 1948 let me tell you of a specially memorable holiday that I had that summer. Dave and Elaine were friends I had made in Hong Kong and they came up to Kukong to spend Christmas with me in 1947. Dave was in charge of Geography at the University of Hong Kong and he and his wife were used to Hong Kong European standards of smartness when it came to Chinese servants and their uniforms. As a bachelor I was quite content with a Chinese who was a bit of a rough diamond but he looked after me well and his wife did the washing. It being winter he served our first dinner in 'casual wear' and a greasy cloth cap that must have gone back to his Australia days where he had gone years before to see if there was any gold left (far too late in the day!). It was the perfect reminder to my friends that they were now in post-war rural China and that we lived a very much down-to-earth existence. They were tickled pink and often referred to it afterwards as a kind of initiation. Fortunately the meal was good. Over Christmas we conceived the idea of Dave and myself exploring China. I had only been as far as Hankow and Kuling and because of the war Dave had not been anywhere outside Hong Kong. China is a big country to choose from but we eschewed Peking and all the show places and plumped for South West China and the wilder country north of Kunming in Yunnan Province. The Methodist Church had a well-established work among the Miao tribespeople in the mountains and I had a number of personal friends among the missionaries with whom we could stay.

We met in Canton and on the second of August left Canton Airport on one of General Chennault's planes. During the war he had commanded the Flying Tigers who flew their aircraft out of

Kunming. Several of these planes were left-overs and very rickety affairs they were after all they had been through. Our plane was an empty shell with luggage and cargo strapped to the floor down the centre of the plane and such passengers as wished to venture sitting on canvas 'bucket' seats fastened to the sides. We were supposed to stop at Liuchow (Liuzhou), the capital of Kwangsi (Guangxi), and the pilot came low down among the curious limestone pillars that are a feature of Kwangsi and are represented in so many paintings by Chinese artists (originally hills and mountains sculptured by rain). There was a fairly heavy mist but I suddenly saw the top of one of these pillared hills alongside our window. The pilot must have taken fright too for he suddenly roared up out of danger and the Captain came out to say that he would drop his Liuchow passengers on the way back. Such was the way in which planes were beginning to eat up even the vast distances of China.

The Kunming Lake with the incredible temples clinging to the precipitous rock faces of the western mountains suddenly indicated that we were almost at our destination. We were met at the airport by Keith Parsons with whom we were to stay. After the humid heat of Canton the air was a treat to breathe, dry and refreshing, not unlike an English health resort. We soon discovered how generous the climate was in spite of (or because of) the altitude. One of our missionaries who had retired to a house out by the Western Hills, 'Uncle' Evans, invited us to lunch and we saw in his garden growing side by side peaches, apples, plums, pomegranates, pomelos, prickly pears and grapefruit and were told that grapes and dates also grew in those parts. Tomatoes you can buy all the year round, green peas three times a year and new potatoes twice! It sounds a sort of Shangri-La but we were not very impressed with Kunming itself. It was an overgrown and rather quaint country town with cobbled roads and lots of cheap-looking but neat two-storey shops with small-paned windows on the first floor which had something Elizabethan about them. There were plenty of horse-drawn carts and still more beggars. In spite of strict Government regulations many were smoking opium which probably helped to explain the poverty and also the fact that some shops did not open until 11.00 a.m.! There had been buses but these had ceased to operate. I suppose Kunming was caught out in that it had been a suddenly important place during the war (the Burma road led to it). Now it was still the capital of the Province (Yunnan) but was feeling the draught.

By contrast we were very impressed by Tien Nan Middle School which had been built during the war by the Church of Christ in China and the Methodist Church. The setting was ideal. The boys' dormitories were in one rocky valley with a stream running through; the girls' dormitories in an adjoining valley. Classrooms and a new block in course of erection were situated where the two valleys met. The playing fields were on the plain which opened out at this point. The 'railway to Burma' went past the school but when we were there it ran no further than the school which was some eight miles from Kunming and in any case it must have been the railway that once went to Hanoi in North Vietnam. The superintendent in charge of the railway was a governor of the school and he ran trains to the school on special occasions.

Our Zion Methodist Church was on a main road and the premises included an Eye Clinic and a Book Room. Street preaching took place regularly on the first five days of each month and the site guaranteed a curious crowd. I could not follow much of the Sunday morning service (in the national language) but the choir was well trained and so young that it afterwards turned itself into a kind of Senior Youth Club. There were a number of educated and very able Chinese in the congregation whom we met afterwards. There were other churches – and much church work of course. We visited the Church Missionary Society Hospital where we bumped into two CMS missionaries from Hong Kong. There was a YMCA and Dave and I were also invited to a Rotary lunch at the Hotel de Commerce. It was a fascinating mix of nations and occupations. A Father Morse (an American Episcopalian stationed at Ichang) spoke and part of the fellowship consisted of community singing. A member of the staff of the American Consulate gave a powerful rendering of 'Jingle Bells'. Fortunately they did not ask us to start up a song that expressed the spirit of England. What is more, I also had two teeth stopped by a German woman dentist, which was a great blessing.

It was interesting to see how local and national Government were getting their grips on society now that the war was over. We found that in Kunming, for example, they were introducing the idea of driving licences. I went with Edward Moody, the Methodist Chairman of the District, to see him take his test. It was a very friendly affair. The Chinese examiner was not sure what exercises to ask him to do. Ted Moody, as a well-brought-up Englishman, was well versed in the matter and between them they concocted a test that satisfied the examiner. In the office afterwards Ted Moody asked if he could make an appointment for his wife. 'How well does she drive?' asked the examiner. 'Better than I do, actually,' was the reply. 'In that case,' said the examiner, 'I can write a licence for her now.' What a pity our Western world cannot be run on such simple and trusting lines! It made perfect sense.

But we had not come to visit Kunming alone. Our main objective was Stone Gateway, a Miao village some three hundred and sixty or more miles north of Kunming among the mountains. And they really were mountains. Kunming itself is 6,400 feet above sea level. The roads we travelled on took us to some 8,000 feet and mountains often rose above that. It's a wild and desolate country, awe-inspiring I think is the word, and yet has a hard beauty of its own which suggests that man, struggling for existence in the valleys or halfway up mountains, is utterly trivial. One day, I suppose, some of the roads will be metalled and Thomas Cook Ltd will run package holidays for tourists but that day won't be until the next millennium dawns.

16 · Among the Miao

The ethnic situation in this part of China had long since settled into a general pattern. The Chinese occupied the best land, which meant the valleys. The Nosu (non-Chinese and with Tibetan links and resemblances), while on occasions able to withstand the Chinese, had been driven into the less fertile parts and the mountains. The Miao (also non-Chinese) were poorer and less assertive than the Nosu and had long accepted the Nosu as overlords. They had become serfs and tenants over vast areas of the mountains. High up on the mountains by careful terracing they grew maize (which was poor) and potatoes (which were good). They themselves were divided into tribal groups, e.g. the White Miao, the Black Miao, the River Miao (the river being the Yangtse in its upper reaches where it runs north). The Miao of Stone Gateway where we were going were the Flowery Miao.

But how to reach Stone Gateway? Buses had ceased to run. The normal way in which people now travelled was as 'yellow fish' on a truck, i.e. the truck carried its normal freight and those who could scrambled on top and paid the driver something for his broad-mindedness. We failed to get a truck. Six days of our precious holiday had gone and we were contemplating getting a train to Chan-Yi (just over a hundred miles from Kunming) where the railway going north at that time ended and try our luck for a truck there. Then suddenly some urgent business cropped up in connexion with our En Kwong Middle School at Chaotung (Zhaotong) and Ted Moody decided he must go up immediately with a senior Chinese teacher. He had a jeep and a trailer and there was room for us. We were to leave at 5.00 a.m., having got up at 4.00, and it was felt to be a useful safeguard if I got up at 3.30 a.m. to make sure that the cook was awake. Under the circumstances I could hardly say no! We made Weining that evening just after dark (about 9.00 p.m.). It was a journey of some two hundred and seventy miles over an unmetalled road and was bumpy in the extreme even though gangs of coolies were continually filling in the pot-holes and indeed making a good job of it. This was the main road north which was planned some day to reach Chungking. In the valleys we passed farms and small villages but later on we had a long stretch at a great height along the ridges of some of the mountains. Time and time again we could see the wrecks of trucks which had toppled over the edge and lay like toys far below. You need to see country like this in order to appreciate the astonishing achievement of the Burma Road in the last war.

We spent the night with Elliott and Ruth Kendall. Weining

was a Chinese town but also very much of a centre for the Nosu. Apart from the pleasant brick church there were Lower, Middle and Primary Schools and a Dispensary. Next day we left the main highway and branched off to Chaotong where, so far as I can remember, the road ended. Certainly it ended for us. We spent a couple of nights with Ken and Peggy Parsons. In Chaotong the Methodist Church had a hospital, a school, a church and an 'institute'. Whereas Weining was well-used by the Nosu, Chaotong was a meeting and shopping place for the Miao, but it was definitely Chinese and under Chinese jurisdiction. It was at Chaotong that I was able to have a brief talk with a Mr Lee. His office was responsible for collecting a new tax that the Chungking Government had introduced after the war and he was having difficulty in getting the money in. I ventured to ask him how much money he was able to send to Chungking each year. His answer was, 'Oh, we don't send money to Chungking; they send money to us.'

On the Saturday (14 August) we finally reached Stone Gateway. It was a glorious ride on horseback of some twenty-five miles over mountain country on a road that was little more than a track. It was also my first riding lesson. We were given a horse each ('mountain pony' might be a better description but I will stick to 'horse'). Mine was called by my own name of Bill. This journey was fairly straightforward but I was to learn later what sure-footed creatures these horses were. They could follow the roughest and the steepest track and a wise man left it to them to decide which way to go. Not having ridden a horse before, I asked for some instruction and was told briefly, 'Stick to the horse and you'll be all right.' I learnt how to sit the hard way by rubbing the skin off a part of me that should not have been touching the saddle at all, but we reached our destination.

The story of Sam Pollard who founded and developed Stone Gateway in the early days is one of the great stories of missionary pioneers. He made a profound impact on a wide area but it was at Stone Gateway that the Nosu 'landlords' gave the church what amounted to two whole hillsides. The original dirty village nearby consisted of a few houses only, but here a kind of model village had been built. We visited a Middle and a Primary School. There was an orphanage and a dispensary and we were particularly interested in the Rural Industry Centre where young men and young women were taught to use simple looms which they could make themselves and, by better spinning, produce far better cloth out of hessian or flax than by their traditional methods. We were taken the other side of the valley to a Leprosy Home which was really more of a hospice. Most of the residents had spent years on the border line of survival, shunned and driven from the villages in their fear of what to them was the disease dreaded above all others. They were, therefore, nearly all in the advanced state of leprosy but here they were fed and cared for and above all else shown compassion. When their turn came they could die with dignity and in a Christian fellowship whether they were or became Christian or not. The astonishing thing was that they were happy and I suppose that it was exciting to have special visitors and to see a couple of odd creatures like ourselves. They sang and laughed and we had a hearty service together in the chapel. We were staying with Charles and Eve Steel who had accompanied us and I well remember Eve putting a new dressing on the foot of a very advanced case. I have a picture of it, in fact, and it was worse to look at than anything I had seen in operations at Kukong or Fatshan. The flies had gathered round and you can't get rid of flies even in England. It was a simple nursing matter in one sense but none the less a demonstration of Christian love that spoke for itself. When we had first arrived we were led through the two ranks into which the residents/patients had arranged themselves by a Mr Cheo who was in charge. He was an educated gentleman and he showed us his Chinese Bible but he would also have had the New Testament in the Miao language. This had first been put into writing by Sam Pollard. Now the 'Pollard script' as it is called has been superseded but it was an astonishing achievement. It looked astonishing too. It had thirty-one consonants and thirty-seven vowels and so could give a fairly accurate rendering of the word in question. It even includes a non-sound. I have a note that an inverted capital V 'indicates a glottal stop which is not a sound in itself but a movement in the throat immediately before making the sound required. It produces a very low guttural'. Like Chinese Miao is monosyllabic.

The most important thing to be said about Stone Gateway is that it is the centre of a wide area where an astonishing transformation had taken place. The poverty of the Miao people over centuries had led to dirt, degradation and immorality. What happened after the coming of the missionaries was that not only were individuals converted but the villages in which they lived were clean and converted too. The Nosu were independent and lived in large ancestral homes which were built as castles. They had no love for villages. The Miao on the other hand were communally-minded and lived together in villages so that a Christian village was something that came naturally to them. As we travelled it was easy to tell a non-Christian village from a Christian village by its very looks and the bearing of the people in it, and by its smell. The baptized Miao had insisted on a very drastic turning-away from past customs. They had cut out of their lives things that seem to us permissible if not carried to excess such as drinking, dancing and the playing of pipes. I was interested to hear that some of the missionaries had been concerned about what seemed to them the probable loss of parts of the Miao culture which had grown up over many years. Could not folk-dancing and the playing of their pipes remain? The answer of the Miao was a definite negative. All these things were associated with the lasciviousness and immorality of their former lives and their retention was unthinkable. However, one brilliant and positive success was achieved by Sam Pollard and the early missionaries. There had been a long-established Festival on a hill near to Stone Gateway on the fifth day of the fifth month each year. It had degenerated into such depravity that it was out of the question for Christians to support it. Could it not be changed into a Christian Sports Day and Festival? It could and it was and it had proved the great annual event in the Miao calendar when we were there. The English religious language has been so drained of its meaning by constant and slovenly use that it is difficult to express what I am trying to describe. In plain English the gospel had been presented (in deed as well as in word) by the early missionaries and the Miao had responded by accepting Christ by faith and had been brought into the family of the church in the power of God the Holy Spirit. Some would call it a miracle. Fair enough!

They invited Dave and myself to preach at the Sunday service with the use of an interpreter. We each did what we could and both were brief. I was also invited to attend family prayers in a typical Miao hut. Family prayers in different people's huts were obviously as much part of their spirituality as worship on Sunday. The floor and the walls were made of earth and the roof was a rough thatch. They had a fire in the middle of the floor and the smoke made its own way out. At the back of the hut was a large recess – a sort of built-in cupboard. After prayers we talked and they produced a crossbow and poisoned arrows which they use to kill animals by way of meat. We were told that some, more up-to-date, had old ramrod muskets. It surprised me that there were any animals to kill and I don't suppose they had much meat in their diet although some managed to keep a few chickens for special occasions. There were also some pigs. When a pig was killed, the whole village would be invited to the feast. Their dress had to be warm. The women wore blouses or wrap-over jackets with hemp skirts which swayed as they walked. Their hair was done up in a cone on the top of their heads if they were married. The men wore a kind of nondescript long gown on top of warmer clothing but had a ceremonial dress for special occasions. While at Stone Gateway we visited the graves of Sam Pollard, who had died of typhoid after many years of service, and of Heber Goldsworthy, who was killed by bandits in 1938. Seven missionary graves at Chaotung were also evidence of sacrifices made in the establishment of the church.

The days sped by happily but we had a problem. How on earth were we to get back to Canton and Hong Kong? We were told that there seemed to be no trucks leaving Chaotung. The only way seemed to be a three-day journey over the mountains to Weining where there was a much better chance. So we set off on horseback carrying our luggage with us. Two experienced Miao guides travelled on their own feet which was a much safer way of journeying. I managed to keep on the faithful Bill but it was not what I would call riding. It was an exceedingly rough track and I nearly plunged over my horse's head every time the track led down into some gully. I paid a price for it, too, and on the second day stuffed my pyjamas down the inside of my thighs to cushion the rubbing. We did about twenty miles that day and reached a Christian Miao village at about 5.00 p.m. It was called Tien Seng Chiao or Heaven Born Bridge because a river nearby disappears into an enormous cleft in the limestone rock. The school lined up to greet us and after we had eaten we were escorted to the chapel for a Welcome Service. It was a service and a half with at least two sermons, several readings from scripture, many prayers and anthems rendered by the school choir and the church choir and, I think, one other. After the lengthy service they carried on singing hymns until midnight.

There was no lying-in next morning as we had to leave early. We did some seventeen miles to another Christian village called Ch'ieh Ch'ung where the school teacher was expecting us. He spoke a little English and did what he could to make us at home – hot water being the most appreciated of his gifts. As the night before, the chapel was our bedroom. When we had eaten we remembered the welcome of the previous night and in view of our weariness we thought the safest ploy was to go to bed. There was a railed platform at one end of the chapel and by using the string we had brought with us we rigged up our mosquito nets in front of the platform, making use also of the odd nail on the side walls. We changed into pyjamas (mine more than a little creased) and settled down for a good night's sleep. It wasn't long, however, before an old woman with an oil lamp opened the door and sat at the back. An old lady dutifully saying her evening prayers in chapel, we thought. But then more came along with their lamps, men and women, young and old. I remembered the place of family prayers in the Miao church and decided that here they used the chapel rather than the narrow confines of huts. It would obviously be wise for us to lie doggo. At this point, however, the teacher came in and said he was very sorry but he had forgotten to tell us that they had arranged a Welcome Service. He came to the mosquito nets to establish which contained Dave and which me and it was quite clear that he was not to be done out of the welcome – nor was the congregation. He took family prayers and then proceeded to say something to this effect: 'Here in this bed is a learned teacher from Hong Kong,' and he pointed to Dave's mosquito net. He then proceeded, 'Here in this bed there is one of our own missionaries from Kwangtung. We welcome them. We are very honoured that they have come to our village.' By this time Dave's bed was heaving with suppressed mirth and relief as he realized that the onus was on me to do whatever might be necessary. I did my best to respond simply and the teacher translated it for the congregation. I think they would have liked to have seen us in our pyjamas and it was not really polite for us to stay in bed but at the time discretion seemed the better part of valour. They were very kind. They knew that 'foreigners' have strange customs and probably thought that we were obeying European etiquette. Soon through the window we could see the oil lamps taking their owners back to their homes. All was quiet and, after an explosive few minutes' conversation, so were we.

We got to Weining next day about 5.00 p.m., having travelled something like thirty miles but the going was much easier. We soon left the mountains and found ourselves travelling through cultivated fields and woodlands. We had had three days of fine, sunny weather and were very grateful. Next day was almost reminiscent of an English Sunday. Service in the church was at 10.00 a.m. In the afternoon we had a Chinese meal given by two nurses from Chaotong in honour of three other guests and they kindly extended the invitation to us. This was followed by the first of a series of Fellowship Meetings. On the Tuesday we managed to arrange transport on a truck as 'yellow fish'. It was loaded with rock salt. It is very difficult to describe what it is like travelling on bumpy roads on top of such a cargo. There were eight of us and a baby. Some fifteen miles out of Weining the driver broke his gear handle. It snapped clean off at the base, something that I have never even heard of before or since. After a long wait a truck came along *en route* for Weining and our driver got a lift with a view to getting a new gear handle in one of the many 'car cemeteries' in that part of China. As ill-luck would have it, we had broken down at one of the high points along the road, probably something over 8,000 feet. We settled down to a very cold night on the rock salt and the poor baby was sick in the middle of us. Dave suggested getting out the little tent he had with him and sleeping by the side of the road but the others would not hear of it. There were wolves around, they said, not to mention robbers. Next morning our driver returned. Sure enough, he had found a gear handle and we went on our way.

We spent the next night at a fascinating little village called Hershiktou or Black Stone, to allow the driver to take his engine to bits and put it together again. He did not want any more breakdowns. It was fascinating because it was market day and we saw not only Nosu and Miao but representatives of many other tribes (more than a hundred have been classified in Yunnan Province) who had come in from the surrounding hills and mountains. Many were armed with a variety of rifles, mausers, knives and clubs and it was clear that the arms were for use if they got involved in trouble. Fortunately they found us fascinating too and were pleased as punch to have photographs taken of them. One had his worldly wealth in the shape of old silver dollars attached to the sling of his rifle. I couldn't make out what his motive was. Was it swank? Was it bravado? Was it a warning? Or was it simply that he didn't have any pockets? In any case, I have a photograph of him and he looks a most pleasant fellow.

Next day we were off again and stopped for some lunch at a place called Hsuanwei which unfortunately gave an opportunity for a crowd of 'yellow fish' to get on board. There were thirty of us when we started but the driver stopped after half a mile and made six get off. We reached Chanyi by late afternoon. It was then the railhead and an appalling boom town built along the main road at one side of the original village. It was the end of the wartime American pipeline. We spent the night there and next morning got the train to Kutsing where we boarded the 8.15 a.m. express to Kunming. This time Kunming appeared to us as a great metropolis, a centre of culture and a market place for the world – but only until we got our bearings. Before we left Kunming for Stone Gateway I had contacted the CATC Airways Office and to my great surprise found that the official in charge had been a boy whom I had taught at Shatin some seven or eight years before. He promised to do all he could to help his old school teacher when he was given a date. I went to him again now and on Tuesday, 31 August, we found ourselves in a modern plane, this time with comfortable padded seats, bound for Canton. By contrast with our slow travel in the mountains we now left Kunming at 11.40 a.m., dropped down at Liuchow at 2.15 and reached Canton at 4.30 (actually 5.30 Canton time).

17 · The Year of the Jitters

This was the year 1949 but troubles really started in 1948. Towards the end of 1948 people were beginning to realize that the Communist armies would take the whole of China and even more certainly Canton and the Province of Kwangtung. We had our own problem in the Methodist Church in that after two years or more of preparation we were about to build a new block for the Fatshan hospital planned to be the first of three blocks joined together like the letter E. It seemed an inauspicious time to start on such a scheme especially as part of the money was to come from an appeal to the business firms of Hong Kong. We had actually begun building because it was clear that, whatever government was in, the hospital (and the new block) would be serving the people over a large area – but how would the Hong Kong firms see it? Several of us were asked to take time off to go down to Hong Kong to approach the firms personally. In those days it was fairly easy to see the head of even the large firms, and we received a sympathetic hearing but it was an appalling time to collect a large sum of money for a hospital extension which people now realized would soon be in Communist hands. We soon saw that it would be a harder task than we had bargained for. The heads of some of the large firms understood why we had decided to go ahead with the building and gave grants but many did not. This meant that we had to contact many of the innumerable small firms and engineer something of a popular appeal. The local newspaper carried the appeal and one or two cinemas agreed to show slides with details. We had arranged with one cinema to be the beneficiary of the premiere of the film, 'Scott of the Antarctic', but this was cancelled when it was discovered that another charity had already asked for this and been turned down. We had a number of disappointments but we pressed on with visits to firms during the day and correspondence at night. I well remember entering the humble office of a company whose name I have forgotten but it was something followed by 'Steamship Navigation Company'. After I had explained my visit the surprised and forlorn-looking Secretary explained that the Company had lost all its ships in the war and that her job was to keep the office open in the hope that some compensation might come along one day. The poor lass! I felt I ought to make a contribution towards the cost of lighting and the making of tea.

The Appeal was master-minded by Donald Childe, J. E. Sandbach and Dr John Rose with Frank Evison, 'Pred' (Peredur) Jones and myself assisting. I went down to Hong Kong three times, in October and December 1948 and March 1949 – fifty-one days in all although I must confess that I found time to visit Cheung Chau and Lantau again, to look up friends and to see several good films in Hong Kong cinemas. We had a letter from the Chinese Chamber of Commerce to introduce and commend us. Apart from church money and this appeal we had grants from several charitable organizations and at least two large grants from the American ECA (Economic Co-operative Administration), but even the ECA almost pulled out of its promised second grant when the prospects of a Communist Government loomed before it.

It came through in the end in December. It was a new experience for all of us and it proved worthwhile. The new wing of the hospital was opened on 22 May 1949 – some five months before Canton fell to the Communists but even so no one felt able to come from Hong Kong in case they were cut off. That's how things were for some months. In fact Mao Tse Tung had earlier announced 19 May as the date set for the 'liberation' of Canton and he went on the air to apologize to the people of Canton for being late!

The jitters, therefore, were well on the way by the time 1949 dawned. What did the future hold? To run or not to run? The farmers and the poorer folk had no choice. They had to stay and the prospect did not look too bleak. The people with a lot of money had moved already. Those with some money had a difficult choice as did the professional folk and those engaged in commerce. In the hospital it was impossible to advise people. They asked us whether we, i.e. the three Europeans, Drs Rose and Austin and myself, were staying. Following the normal missionary tradition not to leave unless things became impossible, we answered them that we were. In earlier troubles this century we had established the precedent of a first stage in which wives and children left. On this occasion the warning from the Consul in Canton that non-essential personnel should return to the United Kingdom did not come until May. In January members of the Chinese staff of the Central Hospital, Nanking, joined us including a well-known eye specialist who ran an eye clinic for us twice a week. They later moved on. The trains from Hankow became more and more crowded so that it soon became impossible to get on them so far down the line. As well as Chinese, European and American business and missionary families came through Kukong, sometimes accompanied by the husband as far as Canton or Hong Kong. When I knew that any were coming on a particular train I tried so far as possible to meet them at the station with refreshments and had to spend many long hours waiting for the train to arrive. So far as the Chinese were concerned it gradually became clear that the only refuge was either Hong Kong or Taiwan (Formosa) where Taipeh was to become the new Nationalist capital.

A particular problem was the Nationalist soldiers. I felt sorry for them because they sensed that they were on the losing side and to a large extent they had to fend for themselves. Church buildings were an obvious target for occupation. We had to do our best to retain them for our own use and in any case we did not want to appear to the Communists that we had been welcoming them. Ying Kwong school, next to the hospital, had them in for some time. We managed to reduce their numbers and reached an interesting compromise that if we left them in peace they would keep other soldiers out. They also kept thieves out! A building, on our side of the river and nearer the town, which had never been repaired since the war and was still little used by us, was often taken over. We had a weak case to offer there but we did have a long-running argument with the military over two massive

97

wooden doors which they had taken away. We finally got them back. Our main city church was occupied several times but we either got it back or came to some agreement about joint use. I remember a Major (or whatever the rank) Lee who arrived with troops on one occasion and who turned out to be a member of the Methodist Church, which put a certain obligation on both sides. I have a great regard for him because after a few days he cleared the church at a time when things were hotting up and it could not have been a popular move with the troops concerned. If I remember rightly he seemed quite clear that he was on his way to Taiwan. In September an officer from the Nationalist 39th Army turned up to arrange for the army to use part of the hospital. We were able to keep them out by agreeing to review the situation in the event of an emergency.

Our District Synod was held each January and in 1949 it was at Fatshan. I was unable to go because I was helping to cope with soldiers but I did attend the Missionaries Meeting which took place when the Synod was over. I discovered that the Synod had moved Huen Fung Sheung, the Superintendent Minister at Kukong, to Fatshan and appointed me in his place. This seemed a retrograde step as we were aiming to transfer all administrative responsibility to Chinese ministers and laymen but a young and able Chinese minister was to be stationed at Kukong. I suppose the political situation also had something to do with it. At the same time I was appointed business manager of the Kukong Hospital in the place of a Chinese who had left because of the political situation. It was an emergency situation and I had to accept it as such although in normal times I would not have qualified for either job! The hospital coolies were unsettled and in March the four water-carriers became so unreliable that we had to dismiss them. Two of the wives who were hospital servants left too. I should explain that we had no running water and the provision of the whole of the water needed by the hospital had to be supplied by these men. It was a crisis indeed. As luck would have it, the servant I had had when I was at language school on Cheung Chau had returned to his village which was not far away. His name was A Wa and he was back farming. He agreed at a few hours' notice to take over responsibility for water-carrying and he

98

took on four local men he knew to take the place of those who had left. This was tremendous relief as he saw to it that there was no more trouble on this front.

The hospital normally lost money during the winter and made up for it during the summer but this January seemed particularly difficult. We had to reduce staff and simplify the Stores and the Accounting. John Rose, who was in general charge of both hospitals, was obviously of great help when he was in Kukong. Bert Alton, who had worked in the North River Circuit in the 1930s and was well known locally, came up for a short time to give some valuable help and support. Frank Evison and Pred Jones, who had been in Kukong during the war when it was in Free China, also visited and gave a hand. The job of a business manager had been created to avoid putting routine administrative work on the busy Chinese staff (doctors, a matron and nurses) and I could not really involve them further, able though some of them were. In February we suffered a serious loss in that the very fine and efficient Matron, went to England for further training. All pressed her to go in spite of the situation and this proved to be the right advice in the long run as she is now a doctor in charge of a nurses' training college in Kukong in what we think was originally our church hospital.

The most persistent difficulty was the currency. The Chinese (Nationalist) dollar lost its value in so dramatic a way that we were using notes valued at tens of thousands, then hundreds of thousands and finally millions of dollars. In August 1948 the Nationalist Government brought in a new currency known as the 'gold' dollar. The value was fixed at three million old dollars to one new. There was, of course, nothing 'gold' about it. A vigorous Black Market followed a shortage of the new notes. In October there was a sudden lack of confidence in the new dollar. Shopkeepers refused to sell and farmers refused to kill pigs or to sell rice. There was a fantastic Black Market in cities such as Shanghai and Canton. The Government shot a few people but that did not help. When it came to the transfer of outside money to China it had to be done through Shanghai. The banks, or perhaps more accurately people in the banks, forwarded the amount of Chinese dollars that the money was worth on the day of receipt but delayed the transfer for some days until the Chinese dollar had sunk further and they were able to buy Chinese dollars more cheaply, sometimes at half the price. Small fortunes must have been made that way. We were involved because we were getting grants from the USA through UNRRA for the new hospital wing at Fatshan. The second of three instalments took three weeks to be transferred from Shanghai and in that time we lost two thirds of its value. The value of the dollar was a daily hot point in conversation. I once attended a service in a village chapel at which the catechist painted a most vivid picture of the poverty-stricken Prodigal Son. He emphasized his plight by quoting the price of rice in the far-off country. I checked afterwards and discovered that his was the accurate quotation for the day. There were no flies on him! In April 1949 the Communist armies crossed the Yangtse and this led to another dive in the dollar's value. Again shops refused to open and we had to 'borrow' meat and vegetables to provide food for the hospital. Then people began producing old Chinese (silver) dollars of pre-war years which they had not exchanged. Other coins turned up. I personally handled a British Crown of King George V, a Spanish Crown of the eighteenth century, a Mexican dollar of the last century and a number of Maria Theresa thalers. The Nationalist Government then produced new silver dollars. All these coins were of silver and they all ranked the same.

The Maria Theresa thaler was an interesting coin. Maria Theresa was Queen of Hungary and Archduchess of Austria and died in 1780 but the coins continued to be struck in Vienna, then in Rome (by Mussolini), then in the Royal Mint in London, then in Bombay (during the last war), then in London again until 1962, when they were discontinued in response to a request from the Austrian Government. They were all dated 1780 and seem to have been used most widely in the Middle East but some obviously found their way to China. To complete the story of the currency, the Hong Kong dollar was always used whether surreptitiously (when banned by the Chinese Government) or openly. When times were particularly bad I remember that we had to accept rice as hospital fees!

It must have been just before the introduction of the 'gold' dollar that I had a visit from Captain Diggens of the British army whom I had met on the road going south from the Queen Mary Hospital in Hong Kong as we were both looking for earth that was deep enough for burying the dead. Apparently a British soldier had died in our hospital during the war and was buried in Kukong. Captain Diggens had been sent to recover the remains for re-burial in a Hong Kong war cemetery. The Methodist church had its own cemetery on the top of a hill outside the city. It was a fine site where we had a dawn service every Easter Sunday among the tombs – a truly joyous occasion as we sang, 'Christ the Lord is risen today'. The Chinese minister looked up his records. Yes, an English soldier had been buried there during the war but he was not sure whether the grave was sufficiently well marked. We had brought two coolies with us who finally agreed to charge two million dollars if they found the body and one million if they did not. It was, as usual with the Chinese, a very sensible bargain. We found the bones which the worthy Captain Diggens put in a sack and we adjourned to the hospital for a cup of tea and food. It was an interesting meeting and certainly an unexpected renewal of acquaintance.

It was in February that the coolies responsible for rubbish disposal (including all the refuse from the wards) discovered a quick way of disposal by dumping it in a recess behind one of the buildings. It is a blessed law of nature that such stuff soon develops a warning smell and we discovered it after a few days. By then it was in a bad state and not a single coolie would touch it. I think that they were genuinely scared of it. However that may be, I had to shift it myself as I repeated to myself over and over again what someone had told me years before that you can't be infected by a smell. It was however a shocking thing to discover in a self-respecting hospital. On the whole though the whole staff from the coolies up were loyal and worked well, but all the time they had to face this nagging question as the Communist armies drew nearer: 'Should I go south or back home or hide in a village?' These choices were all the more real because Kukong, by now itself very crowded, was on the main route (by road and rail) from Hankow on the Yangtse to Canton. Fighting could break out here on a scale that was unlikely in the country areas.

In those months one or two of the qualified sisters left us. In May seven of the students and three nurse aides went back home, which was entirely reasonable. On the other hand, nine new students turned up in August to enrol for the new term. It became a matter of maintaining morale. The discipline of hospital life helped enormously and prayers and sermons in the hospital chapel took on an underlined reality. Special events were arranged. In July John Rose arranged a boating picnic to an island in the river for the Nursing School, students and teachers, where we played softball and ate and drank. It was glorious weather, I remember, and it all helped. In fact we repeated the picnic on the island the following month. In September some twenty of us went by bus to Naam Wa Tsz where there was a famous Buddhist temple. We later heard that the bus before ours had been stopped by robbers and one passenger was killed, but we had no trouble. We admired the trees and gardens of the temple; we took photographs of the statue of the Buddha who looked fat and pleased with life; we gazed with astonishment at a mass of hideous carvings on the wall of the main shrine. We met the old Abbot who welcomed us and some of us (myself included) bought some long-life tea. Like our English cathedrals they had to sell various objects to visitors in order to keep going and their speciality was this tea. When I tried it back home my taste buds told me that it was ordinary 'green' tea spiced with liquorice. We had concerts using gramophone records and film strips as well as local talent and we started organized games twice a week on the playing field of Ying Kwong School. In September we heard that there were Communist guerrillas within fifty miles of us on a broad arc from north to east. 'Communist guerrillas' was a very broad term in those days, so far as I could make out. Some were undoubtedly in touch with the Communist armies but others were having a go on their own account.

On 27 September some Nationalist soldiers turned up and dug two rough machine gun emplacements on the river bank about twenty yards from the main door of the hospital. This did not help our morale but we could do nothing about it. Then suddenly things began to hot up. On 4 October soldiers and local government officials left the city. On 5 October the police ordered martial law. The same day many of the sampans by the city upped anchor and came floating downstream past the hospital, not unlike a flock of birds. 6 October was the Moon Festival. The Nationalists blew up the Kukong railway bridge. Many of the inhabitants of the city moved out to the villages or to the south. We responded by putting on a party that night in one of the classrooms for the student nurses and for all others who were free. It turned out to be one of the happiest parties I have been to. It was partly reaction to the strain we were under but it also owed much to the game of 'winking' which the three Europeans present introduced as their contribution. I suppose that the men present began by guarding the ladies from the back of the chairs but they must have got by for I cannot remember that part. What I shall never forget was the turn-around when the nurses were supposed to guard and steal the men. Not one of the nurses could wink! Someone ought to do some research on this. They went into most fantastic contortions but nary a spontaneous movement of an eyelid that could be construed as a wink. The party became quite hilarious and did a power of good.

18 · The Liberation

That night proved more eventful than we had bargained for. At midnight we heard a sudden round of heavy guns which stopped almost as soon as they had begun. That meant, the Chinese told us, 'We are about to enter the city. Clear out if you are hostile to us.' This time nearly all the remaining boats by the city (many of them forming the bridge of boats) cut loose and swept downstream in complete silence. It was an eery sight in the moonlight. At 3.00 a.m. there was a second volley, this time much nearer. Meantime there was a to-do on the river bank outside our hospital. Members of the police and the fire brigade and others who were in the pay of the Nationalist Government were hurrying by to get out of harm's way but some were evidently robbing boats. Parties would occasionally bang on the doors of the hospital demanding to be let in but the doors were stout and the men were in too much of a hurry to plan a serious attack. We watched those doors throughout the night, knowing that there was little we could do if they got in. Then all was quiet.

At dawn we opened the doors cautiously. Not a soul was to be seen. Then someone who ran a food stall at a spot very near the machine gun emplacements opened up as usual. About 8.30 a.m. two or three Communist soldiers were brought across the river in a sampan and bought some vegetables and perhaps one or two other things to eat. The stall holder was sorry he had no meat! We were liberated. That evening a Chinese minister and I started Bible classes as planned. He had twelve and I had fifteen people – not bad, considering. It had been a most extraordinary day. Indeed it had been a most extraordinary twenty-four hours. We slept well that night.

In the weeks that followed I developed a considerable respect for the Communists. I later made a note of instructions that Mao Tse-tung once gave to the People's Liberation Army (as the Communist army was called) and they were by no means naive or idealistic.

Three main rules of discipline:
1. Obey orders in all your actions.
2. Do not take a single needle or piece of thread from the masses.
3. Turn in everything captured.

Eight points for attention:
1. Speak politely.
2. Pay fairly for what you buy.
3. Return everything you borrow.
4. Pay for anything you damage.
5. Do not hit or swear at people.
6. Do not damage crops.
7. Do not take liberties with women.
8. Do not ill-treat captives.

(Mao Tse Tung, *Selected Military Writings*, second edition, p. 343)

None of us had any rights as individuals by way of protection against the Government as we have in the West and there was trouble if any stepped out of line but the Communists were well organized and reasonable. It was drilled into their troops that they had come to liberate the people and must be friendly and helpful always. It seemed that they made sure that each soldier had money before liberating a town so that they could pay for any minor shopping they engaged in. Their morale was high, as indeed it should have been, now that their victory was in sight, but it was rooted in long years of struggle against both the Nationalists and the Japanese.

The 'Long March' of 1934/35 (see *Appendix C*) was much in their minds. The soldiers we saw in 1949 knew their history and many had been on the Long March itself. Their austere living had survived. Gambling and alcohol were forbidden and as they moved south it had become their proud boast that they always liberated a place on foot – mechanical transport followed. In all this, as in their simple country dancing, they were very different from all other armies in Chinese history and probably elsewhere in the world. Across the river from the hospital ran the railway line and the road to Canton. I found it most moving to watch them marching in an almost continuous stream the hard way to Canton. They started the day after Kukong was taken and they took something like three days and nights to pass. We had various rumours of the fall of Canton but I reckon it must have been on or about 15 October.

Life in Kukong quickly returned to normal. Members of the hospital staff dug a field and planted vegetables to show what good peasants we were (yes, I joined in!). Normal routine had scarcely been shaken. I started what was to be my last Membership/Confirmation class for nurses. We had the occasional concert. On 10 October some army officers came over to inspect the hospital but there was no suggestion of billeting soldiers. The Ying Kwong school was different as billeting officers wanted to put a hundred soldiers in the school for four or five days and as there were only nineteen boys there at the time this was felt to be reasonable. Our City Church premises were inspected and soldiers billeted in the classrooms but nowhere else and they were out in three days. Soldiers need food as well as shelter. They bought pigs and chickens compulsorily but always paid for what they had. I have no note about rice and think they may have brought this with them. They needed wood for cooking and found plenty from what was left of the street barricades that had been put up before their arrival. In the middle of November they imposed taxes. In the city shops it was a tax on sales; in the country farmers had to pay 10%, 20% or 40% of their yield of 'kuk' (rice in the husk) but this was no more, and probably for most a good deal less, than they had been paying under the previous Government. The land-owners who remained were dealt with separately and often harshly. The rich ones had fled. The Post Office began accepting letters once again as soon as 8 October and I received my first letters from the outside on 18 October. The railway was opened again on 25 October, though with breaks between Kukong and Yingtak. On 17 November the first proper train left Kukong for Canton though passengers had to change trains at one bridge. Daily newspapers came in from 11 November. On 24 November the Communist 'People's Dollar' was made the only legal tender and people had to change the old Nationalist paper money at the banks. The new dollar was fixed in terms of 1,500 People's dollars to one silver dollar, which remained as the only piece of money as of value in itself. The People's dollar fell on the Black Market but I have no record of its falling below 10,000, the level reached on 2 December. This was remarkable in view of what people had experienced before. I must also add that on 9 January 1950 the churches of Kukong were invited to send a representative to serve on the town's 'People's Committee'. This also was something that had never happened before.

In the days following the liberation I experienced an almost uncanny feeling in the city which I must try to describe. Everyone was incredibly polite. They were polite to each other and to the Communist soldiers and the Communist soldiers were polite to them. There were obvious reasons. There was relief in that the war was over and that order (if not as yet law) prevailed. There was a feeling of thankfulness that there had been no fighting;

there were probably elements of fear as well. Nothing seemed to be too much trouble to anybody and I began to wonder whether Utopia was here. It was too good to last and I link the beginning of a return to normality with a journey I made to Canton early in December. The front carriage of the train was reserved for the army which seemed reasonable to me as such reservations are common in England. However, a great argument went on between members of the public and the soldiers. What were the soldiers doing in a privileged position like that? They had come to liberate the people. They said they were the people's friends. Let them come out of their carriage and take their turn with the rest. The dream was over – at least for the time being!

Let me not forget to give an emphatic warning to any of you who are ever tempted to smuggle a dog or a cat into this country. Just before Christmas one of the hospital dogs died. The doctors suspected rabies but the symptoms did not fit in with the medical text books. Our senior Chinese doctor obtained permission to travel to Hong Kong with the dog's head for more accurate diagnosis. It was rabies and he brought vaccine back with him. In the meantime two or three other dogs had died, including my own, a half-grown alsatian pup. It seems extraordinary, looking back, that I was with him when he died, trying to get some milk into him. I had begged a spot of brandy from the matron to mix with the milk. He revived for a few minutes and then died. A wit might remark that it was a nice way to go but don't you believe it. Rabies is a terrible disease. We sometimes heard a dog barking or howling the peculiar rabies howl in the world outside. I still listen hard if I hear a dog bark at night. A patient with rabies began shouting in one of the hospital wards when I was taking prayers. He was in agony.

Some weeks later John Rose and I were staying in our Mission House in Canton run by women missionaries. Their cat was lying on a rug when one of its hind legs became paralyzed. We could take no chances. It had to be killed and the only way was to break its neck. It took two of us to hold it down on the rug and the doctor took its head.

Since all in the hospital who had been in contact with the dog were given the vaccine and none contracted the disease perhaps I

107

might sound a slightly humorous note. Drs John Rose and Clifford Austin messed with me in my bungalow and had to be given the vaccine which, to make matters worse, had to be injected daily into the area of the stomach for something like a fortnight. Because I had been away for the critical period of my dog's disease I did not have the vaccine myself. This may be a bit of black humour but I am glad to say that they occasionally managed a wry smile if not a laugh.

We all had a very happy Christmas with services, carol singing, concerts (including one in the Roman Catholic Church), baptisms and an English as well as a Chinese Christmas dinner (not at the same house or on the same day!). Our annual Synod was to be held in January as usual, this time in Canton in a church just repaired after having had its roof blown off when the retreating Nationalist soldiers very inexpertly blew up the Pearl River bridge. The Women's Fellowship of the Canton Methodist Church had been asked by the authorities to help with relief work in the city. They were glad with such backing to open rice-kitchens for the poor and organized a 'catty per person' appeal to raise money. This later seemed to be a pointer to the co-operation between the Government and the churches in social welfare which has been worked out in the 1980s. It was a useful and encouraging Synod. Another Chinese minister was ordained. The traditional 'Missionaries Meeting' had been very sensibly abolished by order of the Methodist Missionary Society in London so we had a 'Meeting of Missionaries' instead, which the Chinese members of Synod did not begrudge us in the slightest. On a more personal note, John Rose and I were to go to England on furlough. It was clear that the Government would not allow me to return as a circuit minister with pastoral charge of churches but it was hoped that I would be able to return to a teaching job.

The building of the new wing of Fatshan Hospital was not the only act of faith in difficult days. The Canton Union Theological College, originally at Paak Hok Tung on the outskirts of the city, had moved to the Lingnan (Christian) University campus after the war where the University had lent it the old silk-worm department buildings. Money had been promised for a new building mainly by the Church of Christ in China and the

Methodist and Anglican Churches. When the Board met at the end of June 1949 the political and economic situation seemed to rule out any possibility of building and it is recorded that no member at the beginning of the Meeting felt that it ought to be contemplated. As the Meeting progressed opinions changed and it was finally decided to build at once. Bert Alton, the Methodist representative and Chairman of the Board, wrote 'I have never before been so conscious of the Holy Spirit taking hold of a body of people and drawing them to an unexpected decision'.

A very pleasant building in a modern Chinese style was put up. The roof was on by the time the People's (Communist) Army entered Canton and classes were being held before the end of November. It was to this College that I might have gone as Tutor but, alas, such a move proved out of the question under the new regime.

For some time the Communist Government recognized the College as a College of Theology within the University, but eventually, some ten years later, closed it altogether. In September 1986 Theological education was restarted in South China, not, however, in this building on Lingnan but in other premises next to the Dongshan church in Canton city. Term began with a full complement of thirty-four students – twenty men and fourteen women.

19 · Farewell China – or Au Revoir?

John Rose and I set about getting our permits to leave China. He had returned to Fatshan and applied from there. Kukong could only give me a pass as far as Canton but they were as helpful as possible. I got the pass within two days together with letters from both the Military Headquarters and the local civilian officials. I had a farewell Chinese feast in a restaurant in the city and next day another at the hospital. It was a sad moment after all we had been through together but for me there was also the excitement of a return to England. I finished packing and on 29 January caught the 'Ordinary Express' which left at 5.30 a.m. and reached

Canton about 2.00 p.m. I was picked up by the police on the platform and escorted to the police station which had an entrance on to the station. Iron gates clanged to and I was alone. It was a peculiar feeling to realize that no one knew where I was and I had no right of appeal to anyone. I had nothing to fear but it was an insight into how people round the world feel when this happens to them – especially in some countries. I had an amicable conversation with the officer in charge. It so happened that in the last day or so the BBC had announced on its overseas service that the British Government had decided to send a *chargé d'affaires* to Peking. I thought it would break the ice if I said how glad I was that my Government had recognized his Government in this way. I felt a little chilled when he replied, 'Yes, but my Government has not recognized your Government as yet.' However, I got safely to Shameen, the old Foreign Concession, where our Mission House was.

Next day I went back to the police station to fill in forms and again the following day to fill in more forms. Among other things I had to submit a complete list of my baggage and all the items in the baggage. Then it was a matter of waiting but we were able to visit friends and exchange news. My permit arrived before John Rose's but it was not wise to wait for each other. On Saturday 11 February 1950 I took the 8.15 a.m. train to Shamchun which is the station on the Chinese side of the border with Hong Kong. There we had to unload the baggage and walk the short distance to the train on the British side of the border. The Chinese officials gave me a most exhaustive search. They took over an hour to examine my trunk and suitcase and two boxes. Meantime I stood with my eyes glued to the heavens not in any religious exercise but simply because one or two Nationalist planes had bombed that station the day before. I could not make up my mind what to do if I heard the sound of planes coming again! However, all was well. I crossed the border and was welcomed by the Rev. A. H. Bray and the China Travel Service.

John Rose arrived a day or two later and we sailed on 17 February for London on SS Corfu. We were in holiday mood as you can imagine and perhaps that was one reason why we joined in the search for the most beautiful girl in the world. Let me explain. A bachelor friend of ours (not, let me say, a missionary) was returning with us and was anxious to meet again a Chinese girl who lived in Singapore or Malaya (now Malaysia). She had obviously bowled him over at an earlier meeting and he was of the opinion that no girl in the whole world was her equal. What could we do but assist him? We had two days in Singapore and discovered that the Chinese family in question lived in Penang, our next port of call. That gave us the opportunity of having a meal with some Chinese friends of John Rose; also to meet Dr and Mrs Amstutz who kindly invited us to lunch and tea at the Mount Sophia Theological College. He was an American Methodist Bishop in charge of an enormous area which included islands far across the seas. We also visited Wesley Church which was the first Methodist church in what was then a colony and came under the Methodist Church of Great Britain. It was good to meet the Methodist padre there and he also gave us lunch.

Then came Penang, a lush and beautiful place, but it was not the kind of beauty our friend was seeking. We found the father, a solicitor, in his office. He welcomed us and, perhaps in order to get on with his work, invited us to a Chinese meal in his home that evening. That evening his younger daughter collected us by car and took us to the lovely home which in those days had an armed guard because it was in the country. She too was lovely but apparently did not compare with her elder sister. Alas! the elder sister was married and in another part of Malaya. It's amazing, though, what good food does. Our friend bore up bravely and enjoyed his meal.

We reached London on 20 March. Remember that at that time we both hoped that we would be returning to China although we knew it was in doubt. So I went to our Missionary Society Headquarters for the routine medical examination, had my typewriter repaired in Kingsway, bought an umbrella at Selfridges and prepared for whatever Providence might have in store for me next.

Appendix A

The Girl from the Mountains
(an account of an operation by John Rose MA, FRCS)

Two frightened and exhausted people arrived by boat at the hospital steps and had the utmost difficulty in ascending them and entering the hospital gate. The woman was using two sticks to keep upright for she had a lump in her abdomen much larger than a volley ball. It was so large that she was unable to stand without support from in front and, on a stretcher, gave the impression of a huge Christmas pudding with matchstick arms and legs. Her body was emaciated and her head was that of an old woman. She was bald, pale and wrinkled. She looked tired out with pain and the strain of the great burden she had to carry. There were only a few teeth left in her mouth but she could drink and eat small amounts. I diagnosed an ovarian cyst as the cause of her ill-health. She was apathetic at first. The outlook was poor, not least because of her starved condition.

With her was a young man who was evidently closely involved. I thought he might be her son for he was most attentive and respectful. When she was safely in bed (one can hardly say comfortably in bed!), I enquired about their history. They lived in the high mountainous range west of Kukong (perhaps three weeks' walk away) and wore outlandish clothes which made our nurses smile. He spoke Cantonese with an unusual accent and had little money. I learned later that in these mountains the customs and dress of the Ming dynasty still survived.

I was forced to operate quickly because the tumour was enlarging daily and the pressure it exerted was literally squeezing the life out of her. She was weighed by fixing a chair on to a stout weighing machine and then lifting her on to the chair – her weight was 141 lbs.

At operation under local anaesthetic the first job was to release the fluid from the tumour. I drew it off slowly and intermittently so that her circulation could adjust. After about an hour the pulse

112

was better and we gave her a general anaesthetic and I opened her abdomen 'from Dan to Beersheba' – an incision more than two feet in length. The skin was paper thin. The cyst appeared to be benign (that is, not cancerous) but partly adherent to all other organs in the cavity. I excised a portion of a villus nature on the sac wall and decided to marsupialize. The largest and widest many-tailed bandages were applied and we used several large rolls of sterile cotton wool to pad the now flabby and hollow-looking abdominal wall. She was returned to her bed, already awake again after light anaesthetic. The man came to sit by her and was her day and night companion. She had no vomiting or distress. The dressings had to be changed very frequently for some days but the fluid gradually lessened. She ate and drank well but was very weak.

After three weeks I removed the stitches and found that the cavity had shrunk dramatically. The skin had improved but was still lying in loose folds. She could now be lifted slowly by two nurses and was turned on her side for periods each day. In about one month she was able to stand with help and her weight was now 68 lbs. We began massage and exercises from this time and gave her nutritious foods. Over the next few months her hair grew again, the lines and creases of her face disappeared, her skin texture and colour showed marked improvement. Some teeth appeared in her gums. Dentition must have been much delayed.

She became a good-looking girl, learned to talk and smile again. She attended services and Bible classes. She was, in fact, not quite seventeen years old and the 'son' was her husband. They had lived as slaves in a feudal household in these mountains. When her illness made her useless to their 'landlord' or owner they were neglected and had 'run' away with the help of his relatives. They had taken some months to reach our hospital.

She became a Christian and seemed to enjoy her long overdue childish games. Her husband did jobs for us about the compound. Her abdomen unbelievably returned to normality and the original incision of about twenty-five inches became a four-inch scar. All discharge dried up. I had anticipated doing a second operation after a year but she returned back up to her mountain village after it had been liberated by Mao's army. I returned to

Fatshan and heard no more of her. She will now be about 57. I wonder whether she has started a Methodist chapel (Ming dynasty style) up there among the tigers in those remote mountain ranges.

Appendix B

A Strange Vision

During the long 'infiltration' of foreigners into China there was an understandable reluctance on the part of the Chinese to sell town sites to them. This was one reason why foreign compounds tended to be on the outskirts. The sale of the land to Wa Ying School (above page 13) was of land that nobody wanted because it had been an execution ground. The renting of a town house in Kukong long before the church (mentioned on page 77) was built, was of property said to be haunted. The detailed story of this was discovered by the Rev. Edgar Dewstoe, Chairman of the District, 1920–1935. After his retirement he told it to me and I put together the following account from notes made at the time:

It was just before the Boxer Rising, possibly 1899 or the later months of 1898. I was living in a house in Bow and Arrow Street (Kung Chin Kaai) rented from a family called Lam and had been on my own for more than a year with just a Chinese servant to look after me. The preacher at the church in those days was Hoh P'iu. I had had malaria on and off for some time and was not particularly fit. In the evening of that particular day I went along to some meeting at the church and returned shortly before nine o'clock. I remember that it was a moonlit night but with clouds obscuring the moon at intervals.

The house I lived in was a typical Chinese-style house with an ante-room opening off the street and the main room further on behind a screen. You will remember that there is usually a red beam stretching across this room a little up from the height of the eaves. As soon as I entered this room I saw a Chinese woman hanging by her neck from this beam. She was well-dressed in an embroidered gown and was obviously a lady of class. Her face and features were so distinct that I could have recognized her in the street any time. She seemed to be about thirty years of age. I was much taken aback and wondered at the time what it was I was seeing. I walked up to her with my

115

hand out to touch her. She remained there until my hand was about a foot away and then vanished. I walked round the room to see if I could recapture the vision from any particular angle, but I could not and never saw it again during the rest of my stay there.

I realized that it would be unwise to talk about what I had seen, but a few nights later I was talking to Hoh P'iu and we got yarning. He asked me whether I had ever heard how it was that the house came to be rented to the Mission. I said, 'No,' and he then told me that many years earlier Mr Lam's youngest wife had committed suicide by hanging herself from the beam in that very room. After that neither the Lam family nor other Chinese were willing to live in the house because of the spirit, but it was rented to 'foreign devils' because they were known not to be afraid of ghosts. I then told Hoh P'iu what I had seen and he agreed it should be kept from my servant and others.

Appendix C

The Long March
(an attempt at a synopsis)

The Long March of 1934/35, evading, skirmishing and fighting
the Nationalist armies of Chiang Kai-Shek as well as facing some
of the cruellest landscapes in the world, will remain as one of the
epic marches of history. The Communist army had its main
stronghold in Jiangxi (Kiangsi) province, 'the Central Soviet
Area', which was threatened by Chiang Kai-Shek's armies. On 16
October 1934, after preliminary movements by way of re-deploy-
ment and diversionary tactics, the main force (later known as the
First Front Army) broke out of the Nationalist stranglehold and
began its march during which Mao Zedong (Mao Tse-tung)
gradually established his supremacy over its various leaders.

They were never able to plan a route far ahead but had to
extemporize as the vagaries of war and countryside and inhabitants dictated. They carried far too much baggage including
heavy guns, printing presses and other impedimenta and most of
this they had to sacrifice in stages. Most of the route they
eventually followed was unknown country to them. The troops
were not equipped for cold weather and food was often scarce and
at times unobtainable. They lived off the country but made a
point of paying in money or kind, often with the spoils of
oppressive landlords who had fled. They were helped by the
fortunate chance that the Nationalists' Radio Code was 'leaked' to
them, a fact that Chiang Kai-Shek never realized until much
later, and they were usually able to pick up the orders being sent
to the Nationalist troops. Their training in guerrilla warfare
meant that by avoiding the towns and cities and keeping to
footpaths and mountain trails, also by their acceptance of night
marches, they were able to move very rapidly to the constant
surprise of Chiang Kai-Shek in spite of his planes. Their greatest
asset was the morale and devotion of the main body of the troops
and perhaps one should add the ruthlessness of their commanders.

117

Their route led from Jiangxi (Kiangsi) along the northern borders of Guangdong (Kwangtung) and Guangxi (Kwangsi) and the southern borders of Hunan. After fierce battles they continued into Guizhou (Kweichow) and Yunnan. Here Chiang Kai-Shek many times thought that he had them trapped but by counter-marching and at one time feigning an attack on the city of Kunming (which caused Chiang Kai-Shek to withdraw many of his troops from further north) they managed to cross the river Yangtze at a part that was called the Golden Sands River. They then turned north into western Sichuan (Szechwan). Here they were in bleak, mountainous country not far from Tibet itself. How they climbed the Snowy Mountains (the Jiajinshan range) in ragged summer clothing and straw sandals and traversed the Great Grasslands, a vast semi-frozen marsh on an 11,000 foot plateau, is vividly told in Harrison Salisbury's recent book *The Long March – The Untold Story*. They then passed through southern Gansu (Kansu) and reached northern Shaanxi (Shensi). Here they found another Communist Army holding a Soviet Base Area and joined up with them amid great rejoicing. It was the end of October 1935. Yan'an (Yenan) was to be their new Headquarters.

In the next few months Mao Zedong was joined by the remnants of other Red armies, in particular the Second Front Army which had arrived from Hunan, having followed roughly the route of the main Army at an interval of some twelve months, and the Fourth Front Army from northern Sigchuan (Szechwan) which had joined the main Army at the Snowy Mountains but left it at the Great Grasslands in an abortive attempt to contact the Russian Soviets by going west towards Xingjiang (Sinkiang) Province.

The Long March came to be known as the '25,000 li March' i.e. just under 9,000 miles (mistakenly said by Harrison Salisbury to be 6,000 miles which in fact represents Edgar Snow's suggested figure of 18,088 li). This must be a gross exaggeration but it is impossible to estimate in any accurate way the twists and turns and counter-marches that were forced on them. It is reckoned that some 86,000 men (and some women) set out from Jiangxi (Kiangsi) in October 1934. Possibly only some 4,000 reached the

North-West but this is only part of the picture. Throughout the March they suffered horrific casualties e.g. 40–50,000 men in the first ten weeks. Only some of the 4,000 had marched the full distance. Many times they had to regroup the survivors of two 'armies' into a new unit. Wounds, sickness and desertions took their toll and, especially in the early stages, they had many non-combatants, mainly porters. On the other hand wherever they went they recruited new men who hoped that a better regime could be built which would put an end to the oppression they had suffered under the old. In his book *Red Star over China* Edgar Snow reckoned that as many as 230,000 men were involved in the whole operation and that losses were in the region of 180,000. This book, however, had the disadvantages as well as the advantages of having been written very soon after the event. The main March is said to have taken 368 days which included 15 days of major pitched battles.

The story of the Long March is a story of appalling suffering and loss of life but enough survived to establish a strong Communist regime in the North-West which later made possible the taking over of the whole country by the end of 1949.